"This book is just like love itself—overflowing with profound, rare, funny, uncommon, and splendidly human moments and insights. It filled me, inspired me, reminded me, and surprised me. Slip between its pages and be thrilled by new perspectives about love."

> —SARK, author/artist, *Juicy Pens, Thirsty Paper, www.planetsark.com*

"If you—like me—have spent a lifetime looking for love in all the wrong places, rejoice: You've finally found the real thing. This book is pure bliss."

> —Stephanie Elizondo Griest, author of *100 Places Every Woman Should Go*

"Karen Sorensen was brave enough to ask, and the results are in. Love is alive and well. It's as exciting, challenging, difficult to find, and easy to feel as ever. Carry this book around with you so you never again forget what makes the world go round."

> —Samara O'Shea, author of *For the Love of Letters*

"Anyone who ever felt at a loss to know just what love is will be charmed and enlightened by Karen Sorensen's brave street-level philosophical inquiry and her hilarious, sobering, and hopeful findings."

> —Carlene Bauer, author of *Not That Kind of Girl*

"Startling and magical. When you read this, suddenly you feel intimately connected to people you've never met before."

> —Davy Rothbart, author of *Found: The Best Lost, Tossed, and Forgotten Items From Around the World*

"Don't miss this book from a woman who literally took to the streets to ask people about love. It will inspire and uplift you."

> —Mary Jane Ryan, author of *Attitudes of Gratitude* and *The Happiness Makeover*

"Delightful, fascinating, heartfelt . . . a wonderful window into what hundreds of people experience about love. Read it and feel more love in your life."

> —**Charlotte Sophia Kasl, author of** *If the Buddha Dated* **and** *If the Buddha Married*

"Karen Sorensen has found a way to explore love through her insightful and intriguing research. Her passion has been shared with the world on her journey to find the true meaning of love."

> —**Janis Spindel, matchmaker, Janis Spindel Series Matchmaking Inc., author,** *Get Serious About Getting Married: 365 Proven Ways to Find Love in Less Than a Year*

"On the streets of New York, a crimson clad love detective rewards her witnesses with a rose. The reader who looks below the celebratory surface of this work—part performance document, part compilation of testimonies of the extraordinary nature of the ordinary—will find that a profound and compassionate impulse drives its persistence. In paying close attention to who we are, Karen Sorensen helps us begin to see who we can become."

> —**Matthew Goulish, author of** *39 Microlectures: In Proximity of Performance*

"If you saw her on the streets of New York, dressed to the nines in her cherry-red Love Research suit, you'd definitely stop in your tracks and succumb to Karen Sorensen's questions. Now she shares many of these love secrets in her new book—it's a must-read for anyone interested in the subject."

> —**Sheryl Oring, author/artist of** *I Wish to Say*

love (lŭv) *n.*

Karen Porter Sorensen

Avon, Massachusetts

Published by
Adams Media, a division of F+W Media, Inc.
57 Littlefield Street, Avon, MA 02322. U.S.A.
www.adamsmedia.com

ISBN-10: 1-60550-359-2
ISBN-13: 978-1-60550-359-2

Printed in the United States of America.

10 9 8 7 6 5 4 3 2 1

Library of Congress Cataloging-in-Publication Data
is available from the publisher.

This publication is designed to provide accurate and authoritative information with regard to the subject matter covered. It is sold with the understanding that the publisher is not engaged in rendering legal, accounting, or other professional advice. If legal advice or other expert assistance is required, the services of a competent professional person should be sought.

—From a *Declaration of Principles* jointly adopted by a Committee of the American Bar Association and a Committee of Publishers and Associations

Many of the designations used by manufacturers and sellers to distinguish their product are claimed as trademarks. Where those designations appear in this book and Adams Media was aware of a trademark claim, the designations have been printed with initial capital letters.

Photos by Alex Solmssen.

This book is available at quantity discounts for bulk purchases.
For information, please call 1-800-289-0963.

This book is dedicated to my brother,
who was the inspiration for Love Research

and

My loving grandmother, Elizabeth Sorensen,
who passed away on
Valentine's Day, February 14, 2009.

Acknowledgments

For teaching me every day about love:

My husband and partner in life

My family: Mom, Dad, my sisters, brother, brother-in-law, and nephews

The McGrady family

My Aunt Karen and Uncle Bill for your generous support of Love Research

OVO (Ian, Chris, Hillevi, Ari, Ruben): To ten years of making small art together!

Ruben Carbajal for your editorial guidance

Chris Talbott, Jordan Rathkopf, and Silent Five Communications for strategic advice on marketing and publicity

Ian Rosenberg for directing my performances

Mary Ann Naples, my literary agent, for believing in this project

Katrina Schroeder, Katie Corcoran Lytle, and everyone at Adams Media for your enthusiasm for this book

My teachers: Matthew Goulish and Lin Hixson

My extended family on all sides

My wild mix of inspiring friends

Everyone quoted in the body of this book

And all the strangers that I met on the street

Contents

What drew you to the book you are holding in your hand?

What are you looking for inside? If I had to make a guess, I'd say it was the word "Love." It's funny isn't it—that such a little word can have such a powerful pull? Love is a word I am drawn to, one that is an endless source of fascination. Are you looking for love? Someone to share your life with? We hear the word constantly and see it everywhere, but at the same time so many of us are searching for it. Sometimes love is elusive and mercurial. It can seem to be everywhere and nowhere at once. I hope you haven't doubted in the existence of love lately, or your own worth if you haven't found love yet. Love does exist. I vouch for it. But I'm not saying I never doubted. In fact, doubt is what led me to start researching love in the first place. There was a time when my whole belief system started to crack and I was terrified that this word/emotion/concept that I had based all of my relationships on was an illusion. But then my doubts about love drove me out into the streets to ask questions and find answers. Inside, you'll hear from some of the hundreds of people I met who helped me believe in love again. I hope they appear to you as you read these pages.

Karen Porter Sorensen

Love Research

> The soul needs love
> as urgently as the
> body needs air.
> —*John O'Donohue*

The search for love links humanity together. It is the only universal language we all speak. Yet we understand so little about love and our emotional potential. Lost and confused after a devastating family crisis, I began interviewing strangers on the street, seeking fundamental answers about love. In the spring of 2002, I set out into this vast uncharted territory to explore, not as a scientist or expert in the field, but as an average person with an urgent curiosity.

Earlier that past fall, my fiancé and I had found ourselves caught in a yearlong loop of a debate.

Me: I'm ready for a change. Let's move to New York.
My fiancé: Why New York?
Me: It's the place to be if you are an artist.
My fiancé: Why is it "The" place to be?
Me: It's the center of the art world in the United States.
My fiancé: Why do you have to be in the center? Chicago is a big city and it's more affordable.

Me: New York is bigger, more diverse, and more dynamic.

My fiancé: Is bigger better?

Me: Well, no . . .

My fiancé: What exactly is it that you love about New York City?

I felt like a relentless New York tourist agent trying to sell it to him, but he wasn't one to be easily persuaded.

He was an Irish citizen, and didn't have his green card, making it illegal for him to go with me. Eventually, we came to a compromise: I would give New York City a trial run and he would stay behind until we could get married. I felt strongly that I needed to follow my dreams so I wouldn't have any regrets in the future. I knew who I wanted to spend the rest of my life with, but at that moment our paths led us different ways. I took a leap of faith with our relationship, believing it was strong enough to carry on even through separation and great distance. It was risky, but I hoped in a short time we would be together again.

When I arrived, the city was still reeling from the shock of 9/11. There was a distinct atmosphere of fear that hung, smokelike, in the air. Distrust was palpable, especially when you took the subway at rush hour. People were vulnerable, and their panic made them more aware of each other. They kept their attention outward on their surroundings in case something might happen again. My friends told me that I had arrived in a *New* New York. Post-9/11, the city had changed. Maybe it was because, as Theodore Roethke once said, "in a dark time, the eye begins to see." This was the intense atmosphere of the city as I started my research.

LOVE RESEARCH HOMEWORK:
Smile at strangers.

Love Research

I decided I would set up a Love Research booth in the parks and public spaces of New York and would entice participants by offering them a single red rose in exchange for answering predetermined questions about love. For each interview I would select five random cards from a deck of fifteen questions. I encouraged people to take their time answering and share as much as they felt comfortable. I didn't speak, tried not to judge, and just listened attentively, which made people surprisingly open. These intimate and fleeting encounters not only gave me an archive of fascinating stories from people of all walks of life, they also forced me to examine my own understanding of love and helped me get through one of the most difficult times in my life.

When I began conducting my love research, the results were illuminating and magical, but I never expected the project would send me on a seven-year journey speaking intimately with hundreds of people from all over the country. The strangers I met have impacted me in immeasurable ways; their words linger, and continue to offer instruction. Their stories are hilarious, powerful, passionate, devastating, and inspiring—sometimes all within the same interview. Their words have shifted my consciousness and expanded my worldview. I hung up a sign with the word *Love* on it and, like a force unto itself, it drew people from every walk of life. Over and over again I heard the search for love echoed in people's answers. It's the common denominator. We are all searching for it or desiring more expression of it in our relationships. Love is an active force that we are all responsible for creating. In his book *The Art of Loving*, Erich Fromm writes, "Love is an active power in man, a power which breaks through the walls which separate man from his fellow men." In these pages, I invite you to break down your own personal barriers and meet the world with a new openness. My hope is that the collected wisdom in this book will inspire you the way I was inspired to both feel this connecting force and rekindle your own hidden capacities to love.

LOVE RESEARCH HOMEWORK:
Conduct Love Research. Ask your friends about love. If you are feeling brave, ask strangers.

Lady in Red

Sometimes you just need the right costume to make something happen. I bought a Love Research suit in an East Village shop. It was bright red. Snug as a glove around the bust with puffed shoulders and flared cuffs, it fit like it was tailored for me. When I put it on, it screamed VALENTINE'S DAY; something a hip cupid wielding an arrow and bow might wear. Everything red came to mind when I wore it: stop signs, cherries, fire engines, candy apples, blood, hearts, and most definitely love. Wearing it stirred up my imagination. I found a fedora to match at a St. Mark's street vendor; cocked to the side it gave me a jaunty, determined look.

You Can't Hurry Love

The first day of Love Research was gray and gloomy. I was filled with dread at the thought of asking a stranger for anything, but being a Midwesterner, I always approach things fairly straight on, which helped me gather my courage. Courage in Latin literally means to *take heart*. So take heart I did. The sky threatened rain, but then the sun cracked through and I left my house to begin. I set out to find someone, anyone, who could tell me something about love. At first the task seemed daunting, like searching for love itself—when you look for it, it can't be found. Over and over again I confidently appealed to men and women on the street for an interview, and over and over again they skirted and shied away.

LOVE RESEARCH HOMEWORK:
Buy a love outfit. Be daring! Wear it somewhere love is needed and let it remind and inspire you to cheer up others and spread the love.

An ill-feeling of desperation spread all through my body; everywhere there were people in groups and I was a lone stranger with a microphone trying to invade their private territories. I stalked around picnicking friends, children playing, and couples holding hands. It was impossible to approach anyone.

I noticed a man at the entrance to Prospect Park holding a clipboard for a cause as he pleaded for signatures from every person passing by. Trying to solicit from a stranger is a delicate operation, and I noticed his tactic was far too bold and aggressive. New Yorkers are schooled in the fine art of saying no. They spend their days saying

NO to panhandlers, NO to street vendors, and a big NO to proselytizing religious fanatics. It seemed like New Yorkers were now bundling me into the same category, and it's hard to blame them. I wanted much more from them than their small change: I was asking them to bare their hearts. So I decided I would try a softer, gentler approach.

Finally, I asked an elderly black woman sitting next to me if I could ask her two questions. She agreed. I asked her, **Where did you see love today?** and **What do you love?** She gave me two very succinct responses. I thanked her, and turned off the recorder, but she kept talking.

She told me, "I wanted to buy a rutabaga at the farmer's market but I let it go because my arms weren't strong enough to cut it." I listened, so she continued talking neighborly about the unusually warm weather and her upcoming holiday, "I'm heading to Atlanta, Georgia, to see my son, it's been far too long since we've seen each other." She smiled pleasantly and waved goodbye. I waved back and turned hopefully to ask an older gentleman near me if I could ask him a few questions about love, but he just sadly shook his head and walked away.

> Love is an act of courage. The true revolutionary is guided by strong feelings of love.
> —*Che Guevara*

I Let a Song Go out of My Heart

When attempting an interview, the rejection was the worst. I learned that when pursuing love—or love research—you can't appear desperate. I had to find a way to draw the public to me, something that New Yorkers would respond to, a little bribe, a touch of quid pro quo. I changed my tactics and set up a booth with a bouquet of roses. I sat in silence and let a sign declaring "*Love Research*" speak for me. The simple message stopped busy New Yorkers in their tracks.

Stranger: What's Love Research?

Me: I am researching love on New York City's streets. Do you want to participate?

Stranger: What do you want me to do?

Me: Simple, I ask you five questions about love, you answer; in exchange I give you a flower . . .

Believe it or not, it worked.

LOVE RESEARCH HOMEWORK:
Interview experts about love. Ask a cardiologist to explain how the heart works. Ask a scientist to explain the chemistry of love.

The Deck

What questions was I so interested in finding the answers to? Well, I was pretty lost so there were many. I decided to create a deck of cards encompassing questions on all the aspects of this emotion. I wanted to discuss the subject broadly and deeply: from the intimacy of romantic love, to the emotional closeness of familial and platonic love, to the devotion one feels for their country, to the oneness of religious love.

What is love? (Define it in ten words or less.)
Where did you see love today?
What do you love? (List what you love in two minutes.)
What is your current relationship to love?
Who are your love heroes?
Who taught you love?
Have you ever been without enough love?
Have you ever fallen in love? Describe the process.
Do you love yourself? (Were you born this way or did you have to learn how?)
What is the biggest risk you have ever taken for love?
Has your love ever been tested?
How does one prepare for love?

Do you think you have the potential to love more deeply? What would that require?
Do you love America?
Do you think love is increasing or decreasing in the world?

Now that you know what I'm asking, you're probably wondering what would motivate a person to dress in a red suit, plop themselves in the middle of a New York City park, and ask strangers to reveal their most private and personal feelings? Well, let me start my story by telling you about the love in my family.

> The lover of life
> makes the whole
> world into his family.
> —*Baudelaire*

Love Is . . .

I t's funny; you don't choose your family. Biology chooses for you. This cluster of people gathered under one roof—only chance determines who you end up with. Each family is its own unique entity. Unified under a household, each member becomes something bigger than his or herself: a superorganism like a colony of ants or hive of bees. My family was the group I was assigned to. I knew I was lucky. I was grateful to be in the mix with people who shared my quirks and funny ways. I came happily into the world and found my cozy place among them. I was the second of four children and I worshipped my oldest sister, and treasured my younger brother; we all adored my little sister. My parents were an inspired and eccentric, but slightly overwhelmed duo. My dad read philosophy, grew orchids, and flooded the backyard every winter to make an ice-skating rink. My mother wore a crown of braids on her head like a regal immigrant from another era and spent her free time painting portraits in the basement. One time she dug a hole in the front lawn to make a wildflower garden, shocking all our neighbors. My parents used their natural-born creativity and quirks, to teach us that there are a myriad of ways to express love. They loved us wholeheartedly and showed us this by encouraging us to be expressive and unique in an accepting, safe, and creative environment. We were a close-knit clan and shared many interests: art, poetry, music, theater, and the natural world. We all had curious minds and collaborated on creative projects together. We baked, made up songs, wrote plays, made art, and did science experiments. Looking back, I realize creating things together was a way we expressed love in our family.

Family Dinner

Growing up, my parents insisted on candlelit dinners, and every night we sat down as a family at the table. Today, most people don't take the time to sit down together for dinner, but for us it was a way to reconnect, to show that we cared enough to want to know what was going on in each other's lives. To my parents, family dinner was sacred and my father enforced strict rules. We couldn't even answer the telephone. If someone came to the door, he would get up and tell them that we were eating. The table was always set with a tablecloth and candles and each dinner was a distinctive and special occasion. As a kid I sometimes found the formality of this family ritual a bit tiresome. We would complain to our parents that no other families ate dinner like this; when we had meals at our friend's houses it was much more casual. Most didn't sit down as a family. Everyone ate at different times, sometimes even while watching television, scooping their dinner from TV trays. However, looking back now, my fondest memories are those dinners. It was a comfort at the end of the day to sit around the table together.

During dinner, we would talk about the day, and my dad never failed to compliment my mother's amazing cooking. Mom was unafraid of trying new and unusual ingredients and ethnic recipes. Back then in Wisconsin, anything that wasn't a casserole was considered exotic. She always prepared meals so lovingly for us. The warmth and time my mom put into her home-cooked dinners was a way for her to express her love for all of us. Now as an adult, coming home from work, I often eat frozen meals and I miss the family communion. As a busy woman, I'm astounded how she managed, as a mother of four who worked full time. After dinner, we played games like charades, or twenty-one questions at the table.

LOVE RESEARCH HOMEWORK:
Share a meal. Make it an occasion.

The Family Sitcom

Friends used to call our family the Brady Bunch, and were a bit in awe when they visited. They used to say that coming to our house was like going back in time. We didn't seem to be a twentieth-century family, we were retro, something that they'd only seen on TV or in black-and-white movies. Unlike most kids, my parents were still married and liked—even *loved*—each other. They were also in the house all the time, and involved in our lives, *like the Cleavers*, our friends said.

In the small house everyone was in your business and involved intimately in your daily life. There wasn't a lot of privacy, so our lives unfolded messily on top of one another. Poet John O'Donohue wrote in his book *Anam Cara*, "Each person is the custodian of a completely private, individual world"; in my family we sometimes shared that private space with one another. Actually everything was shared, including two bedrooms for four kids, because there wasn't a lot to go around. The rooms were an organic tangle of things, making it difficult to claim private ownership of anything. My older sister and brother sometimes tried to stake out private space for themselves, but I embraced the collective spirit because it gave me free rein to borrow everything I coveted from my older sister. I drove her crazy, always crossing into her territory, poking around the cabinet where she kept her prized possessions, and digging into the depths of her closet. I was an awful pest, often breaking things and secretly wearing her clothing. Years later, much to my chagrin, my little sister did the very same things to me. But because we were so closely connected to each other physically there was a profound feeling of togetherness.

My parents also raised us to take care of one another. From oldest to youngest we kept a lookout to make sure nothing went wrong. When I think of my family, and love, I think of those little Russian dolls that fit one inside the other so neatly. My parents reminded us that each one of us was part of the whole, so we had to pull our share. As children we learned responsibility, but as teenagers we rebelled, fleeing from the house and family, as we went off to redefine ourselves. But now as an adult I can see clearly that my upbringing taught me invaluable lessons.

This notion of family has shaped my views on love and continues to inform how I relate to people in general. By knowing my siblings and parents so well, and because we were always looking out for one another, I learned everyone was an irreplaceable part of the interconnected whole, and together we were something bigger than our individual selves. No matter how far away we went or how much we rebelled, we were a family and remained closely connected to one another.

The love that bound us in our small house continued to bind us together wherever we went or whatever happened in our lives. That love held my family together even during times when love didn't seem like it would ever be enough.

LOVE RESEARCH HOMEWORK:
What are your earliest memories of love? Write them down and reflect on how those memories have shaped your life.

I Fall to Pieces

Shortly after my arrival in New York, my closely connected family fell into crisis when my brother was diagnosed with a mental illness after a series of catastrophic episodes. A manic high propelled him forward like a super human. The chemicals in his body made his mind race. He stopped sleeping and eating regularly as he accelerated to a faster speed. He could literally run up mountains. Several times he spiraled out of control in public settings, and the authorities took him into custody to be hospitalized. But the most frightening aspect of his illness did not become apparent until I saw him face to face.

First Impressions

Seeing him for the first time was a shock. I knew my brother as a handsome, charming man with cheeks that dimple when he smiled. He had long eyelashes, and a warm, lively spirit. However, when he walked through the front door, I knew he was not himself. He had stopped taking care of his appearance and looked disheveled. Silently shuffling into the living room, he stood with military-like attention against the wall. He seemed unable to relate to any of us and wouldn't allow me to touch him. My parents, who had taken early retirement from their public-teaching jobs, sold their house, and moved from Wisconsin to Colorado to help him recover, had grown accustomed to this new behavior and developed a strange casualness as a coping mechanism. They made small talk and invited him to play a game of cards. Somehow the tactic worked. The rules of the card game briefly grounded him into their shared reality and gave my parents hope that someday his old self would come back to us.

I couldn't mask my uneasiness so well. As soon as I saw him, my defenses went up, because it seemed like his body had been taken over by aliens. I couldn't read his facial expressions, so I rambled on and on to escape his silence. Once talkative, he now had nothing to say. I asked him lots of questions that he answered in a monotone. I told him I loved him, like I had so many times before. But this time was different. Illness had changed his perception and he didn't respond in the comforting way that, over the years, I had grown accustomed to.

Me: I love you.
My Brother: I don't believe in love anymore.
Me: Why don't you believe in love?
My Brother: *Love* isn't real.

Me: Love exists.

My Brother: It's a construction everyone fabricates, a shared societal sickness.

His emotional detachment shook my foundation. We had always been able to talk about everything under the sun effortlessly. We shared a vision of the world. Because my brother is extremely bright and unusually perceptive, I always listened closely to his ideas. Now he had gone off alone to some dark unexplored nether region in his mind and had returned with terrifying new insights. A crack in my belief system began to form. What if he was right? *What if love was only a shared illusion?* How could something so solid alter in him overnight? He was making me question the one thing that had given me security throughout my life. I was going to be married in a year, and suddenly I doubted love's power.

The questions that sprung from my brother's insight began to accumulate. They harassed me like a swarm of angry hornets, keeping me awake at night. I desperately needed answers to prepare for this profound life-changing commitment. Facing a year of separation from my fiancé, and full of big questions in a strange new city, I decided I needed to tackle the problem directly. Now, I know asking strangers for answers about love and recording their answers is not the way most people would choose to deal with an existential crisis. If you're a performance artist, however, it makes perfect sense.

The Art of Love

I had been a theater major in college, but took a performance art class for fun and was hooked. The only rule in making performance art was it had to involve four basic elements: time, space, the performer's body, and a relationship between the performer and the audience. In simple terms, performance art could be anything I made happen in a particular time and place. For me, performance was much more exciting than traditional theater because I got to be the creator. Eventually I went to art school for a wildly impractical master's degree in performance art. My studies involved two years of exploration into the avant-garde; sometimes naked, buried in mud, or howling like a coyote on my hands and knees, I learned how to engage audiences and reveal something they had never seen before.

So it was only a natural progression for me to envision a community art project where I would interview people on New York City streets to search for the meaning of love. I hoped that, through this process, I would come to a new understanding and

> Where there is great love, there are always miracles.
> —*Willa Cather*

that my project would have a ripple effect. By focusing my energy on love, maybe I could generate a little love in the world; if I was lucky, maybe some of it would find its way to my brother.

LOVE RESEARCH HOMEWORK:
Spread love graffiti on sidewalks, walls, and bathroom stalls.

Describe the process

I Wanna Know What Love Is

A year of researching love had passed. It was Valentine's Day and unusually warm for that time of year, so Union Square was a hustling whirlwind of humanity. My booth, located in the very center of the city square, called attention to itself with a bold sign that said *Love Research*. I sat at my station dressed in my crisp red linen suit with a matching fedora and waited for strangers willing to speak frankly with me, one-on-one, on the topic of love. The roses I was giving away attracted people like a magnet.

The Language of Love

A precocious five-year-old boy with an accent came up to me, pointing to the flowers and said, "My grandma wants to know how much they cost." I told him that they were free, and I would give a rose to anyone who answered five questions about love. I said, "Can I ask you some questions?" He turned bright red and shook his head. He rattled something off to his grandmother in Russian. She laughed brightly and spoke back to him. "My grandmother agrees to answer your questions if you give her a flower," he said. I handed him a card from my deck of fifteen questions, **Have you ever fallen in love? Describe the process.** The little boy made a disgusted face, but asked his grandmother the question in Russian. She talked animatedly for an infinite amount of time; he looked a little lost, turned to me, and said, "She loved my grandpa. She says they go to fish. Grandpa loved fishing so then he married her." The old woman laughed. "That's all." She proceeded to answer all five questions in expansive narrative detail, which the little boy uneasily translated into tight little compact English sentences. I handed them each a flower and they walked happily away together.

Hours later, I was interviewing a married mother with soft brown curls and a vulnerable face who painfully confessed she was having an affair. I was a stranger, but I was the first person she told. She had a two-year-old daughter and couldn't decide what was best for her. Should she stay with her husband for her daughter's sake or leave her husband for another man she loved? She told me that every morning the first thing her child said when she woke up was "I love you, Mommy." Her eyes welled up because, to her daughter, love was just that simple. She brushed her tears away quickly and when I tried to hand her a rose she wouldn't accept it. She thanked me for the interview and then silently wandered off.

I noticed a handsome man waiting patiently to be interviewed. He had dark hair and shadowy eyes. I shyly handed him a card that read, **Has your love ever been tested?** He hesitated, but then his words spilled out. "I was married—and my wife committed suicide, I felt that her suicide was an absolute test of our love." He sighed. "I went through a lot of anger toward her because I felt she abandoned the love I had for her . . . . When she broke our contract of marriage, I lost faith in what we had." We stared at each other silently, overwhelmed by the rawness of his answer. "I have since learned to regain faith in the human spirit and have got back the hope that I will find love again." After the interview I handed him a rose, thankful for his story. He parted gratefully, like a burden was lifted in telling it.

A flock of African American high school girls dressed in matching basketball uniforms huddled around me joking and admiring the flowers. Each teenager wanted a rose. They lined up, one by one, telling me about their love life. The girls didn't expound too much, but they all shared the same love for basketball and women;

they were all exploring their sexuality. I asked one girl, **What is the biggest risk you have ever taken for love?** She said, "Well, this is my first relationship as being gay. I guess I did take a big risk, 'cause some of my family, they are religious, so they don't understand why I would do that. But she loves me, and I love her, and that's all that matters to me." I was impressed by her calm self-assuredness. After I interviewed each and every one of them, the pack of girls took a dozen roses in their hands and traveled together down the street.

An African American teenage boy made brazen by attitude approached me with several of his friends in tow. In an aggressive tone he said, "I *want* a flower, how much do they cost?" I told him they were not for sale, but I would give him one if he answered a few questions. Angry and nervous, he pushed, "Just give me the flower." His laughing friends insisted he answer a question. I asked him, **What do you love?** He gave me a blank stare, took the microphone, and said in a dull voice, "I don't love nobody. That's it. I'm done." I was taken aback, hearing truth in those words, but then I looked at him standing there awkwardly waiting for a rose and said, "But why are you

> [Love is] a fundamental human drive. Like the craving for food and water and the maternal instinct, it is a physiological need, a profound urge.
>
> —*Helen Fisher*

answering my questions? You want a flower, and you must be giving it to someone." His friends all burst out laughing, and slapped his shoulders as he walked away resolute, rose in hand.

From behind me, an indignant wiry cowboy with graying hair stumbled up. In a thick southern accent he said, "Well, gawd, seems like everywhere I look everybody's hitched but me, specially here in this park." Interested in learning more, I forgot the deck, and asked him directly what he could tell me about love. He raged over the fact that he was deeply in love with a stripper who lived in Mexico. They couldn't afford to live together. She lived with her family and he was trying to save up to bring her to New York. He told me their love was so pure it put everybody else's love to shame. "I got to tell you, it pisses me off, because, we truly love each other, you know, in a way I don't see anyone else lovin'. And, uh, we don't even have a chance. It's like God said, 'Screw you. Screw your love.' And we can't even be together. We don't even have a *bed* together." The question riled up the cowboy, but he took the rose and walked away with purpose.

A Place for Love to Sleep

That night and many nights after, I remembered the cowboy's words. I thought about what he said, especially when I climbed into my single bed in Brooklyn, longing for my fiancé as I drifted off to sleep.

Throughout the entire year of separation I had felt an ache, like there was a hole in my heart. Had this year apart actually been my idea? I was frustrated with myself for coming up with such a crazy, impulsive plan. I had spent years searching for the right person to spend my life with, and now that I had finally found him, here we were living apart. However, there were important reasons that made me choose to move to New York on my own. At the root of my decision was the desire to fulfill some of my own dreams.

For several years I had been daydreaming about moving to the city to join OVO, a nonprofit organization my friends had formed to collectively fundraise for and produce collaborative art projects. I had been struggling to create art on my own and it seemed like an opportunity I couldn't miss. Even though I loved my fiancé madly and wanted to share my life with him, I needed to do something for myself. I felt that I had fallen so head-over-heels in love that I had lost my own sense of direction in the process. I had placed my happiness in my lover's hands, and it made me feel a little off-balance. I was torn but knew my relationship would be stronger if I fulfilled some of my personal desires.

> 66 In the act of loving, of giving myself, in the act of penetrating the other person, I find myself, I discover myself, I discover us both, and I discover man. 99
>
> —*Erich Fromm*

Still, for all my good reasons, when we were actually apart, it didn't feel like it made any sense. I missed him terribly and I wanted him to join me as soon as possible. As I thought about how much I missed my fiancé and what I had given up to move to New York City, I kept coming back to the story about how we met, and I realized just how important falling in love was for me. I also wondered how important the act of falling in love was for others.

LOVE RESEARCH HOMEWORK:
Turn your bed into a sacred place.

Falling in Love

> ❝When you love, there is neither the 'you' nor the 'me.' In that state there is only a flame without smoke.❞
>
> —*Jiddu Krishnamurti*

When I was working toward my MFA in performance at the School of the Art Institute of Chicago, I spent a summer working in the career development office helping students find jobs and art grants. Across from me sat another grad student who managed the "student affairs" desk, which meant scheduling counseling appointments for undergraduates to talk about their psychological problems. Since art schools are heavily populated with angst-ridden artists, he kept very busy. He was a red-headed painter from Northern Ireland with an accent as thick as a rope. I could never catch everything he said and was always asking him to repeat himself. He wore round glasses and black clothing and had a lightning bolt tattooed on his middle finger. I don't remember the first day we met, but I'll never forget the first conversations we had.

It was like falling into a river of words; subjects flowed back and forth between our desks. From the role of the artist, to Celtic mythology, to political theater and poetry—each stream-of-conscious topic led us somewhere else. It felt as though our souls were speaking directly to one another without barriers or limitations. Talking to him was intimate, and immediate, and reminded me of the late-night conversations I had as a teenager. The kind that would ramble and deepen, and made me feel like our souls were melding. I loved everything he said and took notes in my journal so I could remember his thoughts. He always made me dig deeper, think harder, and look for what was truest in myself. I felt an unusual sense of certainty that he was the person I was meant to be with. All the fibers in my being said *Yes*.

As the days passed, I had the sensation that I was physically changing form; passing from a solid being into a vapor. I was no longer contained. All my hard edges and boundaries dissolved until I was something entirely new. It was like being a child again with no sense of being separate and apart from anything in the universe. I watched the sky and felt myself becoming the sunset. I overflowed my brim. I let go of all thoughts about the past and future and there was only now. Now was magic, unlike any other moment I had previously lived.

For months I had been in an existential crisis agonizing over the possibility that we are alone in the

> "Once happened nowhere else, imagine now."
> —*E. E. Cummings*

universe with only our ego and empty desires to keep us company. Now, the readings of Lacan and Freud in my brutal Feminist Art History class no longer troubled me; psychoanalytic theory seemed insignificant compared to this feeling of oneness and universal flow. The hinges on the doors to infinity opened. *I was in love.*

I became obsessed, thinking about him all the time. Like a fool, I pursued him recklessly, and he seemed interested but elusive. We exchanged love poetry—Rilke, Yeats, Neruda, E. E. Cummings—but he still didn't ask me out. So I went to every one of his art shows, by myself, taking strange bus routes all over Chicago. Each time, I arrived awkwardly and stood staring at one of his paintings until he came over to greet me.

One night at the beginning of the fall semester, when I had nearly given up, it happened. After his opening, he invited me for a late-night dinner date at the Earwax Cafe in Wicker Park. Later we took the L train holding hands, jumping off at random to find ourselves in the Civic Center Plaza. At the center of the Loop's quiet square was Picasso's infamous unnamed statue. When it was erected in 1967, it created a wave of public controversy. People didn't quite know what to make of it, and since it was untitled it held a bit of mystery. Newspaper columnist Mike Royko wrote that it looked like a predatory insect with eyes that are "pitiless, cold, and mean," although he said the "big, homely metal thing" captured the spirit of Chicago—the brutal cops, the slum owners, Al Capone, and the drug dealers. Other

Chicagoans said that it resembled a horse, a baboon, or an Easter Island statue. In my Art History class I had learned that the monumental fifty-foot-high steel statue of an abstract head was either a portrait of Picasso's wife or his beloved Afghan dog. The ambiguity of the abstraction gave it a bizarre humor. Picasso was in his eighties when he was asked to design the sculpture, and despite the fact that he never visited the city, the sculpture has become a symbol of Chicago and a beloved landmark. Without a person in sight, we climbed into its center. With that mysterious abstract animal staring down on us, we had our first kiss. The moment seemed an eternity. The lit city was empty that night, and it felt as though we were the only two people in the world. We spent the night together, and in the morning it was clear to me we would always be together.

street dictionary

🐍 Have you ever fallen in love? Describe the process.

Falling in love is akin to losing one's mind. You feel like you have a great big hole open in the middle of you where everything just disappears inside including your sanity, your sense of direction, and your sense of self.

—*French Woman*

I think falling in love is almost like being possessed. It's a feeling that takes over your body and your mind. If it's true love, it brings out the best in you. You feel like you are completely connected with who you are. It makes you feel like being the best you can be. That's when I think you know you are in love.

—*Possession Man*

He: The process is you lie down on a train track and let the train run over you.

She: Everything that normally makes sense and everything you think you should be doing or shouldn't be doing you kind of ignore.

He: Logic . . .

She: Logic goes out the window.

—*Love Duo*

It's a really wet feeling between your legs. You salivate through every orifice of your body.

—*Bold Woman*

I have been very fortunate to have fallen in love. I think the falling in love was unknown to me, which is unusual. One day you suddenly realize you are in love with someone and that you had ignored the process that was going on for a long time. . . . I think it is unlike any other feeling. In fact, an intellectual friend of mine who is spiritual said she tried to come to terms with the concept of God. The only conclusion she came to after many years of reading texts in many languages was love. Because love was something that the body didn't need to function, therefore she thought *God is love*. It's not something that is necessary for our physical existence but it is necessary for our emotional and psychological existence. It is a divine process and we are lucky to have it.

—*Carol, an Art Conservator*

I've fallen in love a couple times, but probably the most lasting one was my husband where it was love at first sight. It was something that really surprised me. I was definitely not looking for it—it was just sudden. It was the feeling of life changing in like thirty seconds (snaps fingers).

—*Maddie*

Falling in love is like getting hit by a ton of bricks.

—*Honest Woman*

Yes, I have fallen in love and I'm not sure what the process is. I didn't realize I was in love until I was already there. It's kind of like not knowing you fell out of an airplane—until you hit the ground.

—*Falling from a Plane Woman*

Yes I have fallen in love and I'm from the Anvil Drops from the Ceiling School of falling in love. I look at someone for the first time and fall in love at first sight. I just look and Bingo. That's my process, very quick.

—Bingo Woman

I have fallen in love, and it's like you're swept off your feet. You're flying like a cliché. It's intense; it's probably the most intense thing you can experience in your life.

—Swept Off Your Feet Woman

Well, sometimes it's like shopping. You don't know what you're looking for, but when you find it you know it.

—No Bullshit Man

When I was in high school, I fell in love with a drug addict just as I was trying to quit hard drugs. He drew me in deeper and deeper into the relationship. I was trying to be that loving force in his life, which he didn't have from any family members. He didn't have parents, and I tried to be that love for him. I was in love with him, but the more I fell in love, the more pain it ended up causing because he died of a drug overdose in December. I have fallen in love, but then again I was under the influence of drugs and I fell in love with a drug addict. I'm sure the next time I fall in love it will probably be deeper and purer because drugs won't be involved.

—Glittery Eyelids Girl

Love kind of surprises you when it happens. I just remember that feeling, the fact that suddenly that person was on my mind all the time. I was pretty much taking care of myself doing my thing—and suddenly this person is there. So falling in love is exciting. You forget yourself and the world for a little bit. When you're falling in love nothing else matters except for the two of you.

—Wandering Woman

Intense feelings of connectedness, laughter, glowing, warmth, swelling, true focus, huge leaps, confidence, enormous blue sky, fear of loss, time away, longing, seeking, hoping, connecting again, dancing and laughing, bodily joy, home.

—My Elder Sister

Yes, so many times but it never worked out. I try everything; I try to help her with her homework . . . she turned me down. Ask for a dance, she turned me down. I never give up.

—Hope Boy

The process can take five seconds or five years. I mean it's an incredibly vulnerable feeling that suddenly this person—this stranger—has your happiness in their hands. That loss of control can make you feel incredibly vulnerable. I think it is also a hysterically funny process especially in the beginning stages because you may not know the person at all at that point. It's an illusion, your projection, or your fantasy of what you think this person is.

—Homay

Yes I have fallen in love with a beautiful young woman. The process is strange because you don't really realize that you're falling in love while you're going through it. It is sort of like the girl in *Alice in Wonderland*, as she falls down the rabbit hole it's sort of like that. You find yourself falling and you just let yourself go with the flow and you go along with it. You find yourself wanting to spend time with the person and you're thinking of new ways to do cool things, you know, to keep their attention and so on and so forth. It's a cool thing, a cool process when it goes down. It's a fun, beautiful thing, Love.

—Young Spike Lee

I was always thinking about her when I woke up or went to sleep. Anything I did she was always on my mind, so I knew I was in love.

—Latin Deep-Voiced Man

It definitely catches you off guard. There is a loss of self because you are now becoming merged into someone else. You start thinking about "We" as opposed to "I" . . . it makes you feel a kind of surging in your bones and skin. You just feel more vibrant and more alive.

—Entwining Woman

Discovering my soul mate, as she discovers me. At the moment we fell in love we existed as a new, unique entity.

—My Dad

You're in somebody's presence and every glance is an interaction even if you haven't spoken words yet. You can fall in love at first sight by looking into someone else's eyes. . . . You have a first glance, and then a conversation. There's energy, something's exchanged that can revitalize you. Falling in love is a renaissance by definition—it's a reawakening. You view the world in an entirely new way by interacting with this person. . . . Being in love is about being energized and being in awe again. For me living is all about finding reasons to feel awe for life. Love helps you appreciate again.

—*Sophie*

It happened one morning. I woke up and realized I had been in love for a long time. I just knew that was it. It's something very instantaneous. It just strikes you and you know.

—*Rapture Man*

I remember when I realized I was in love—it was kind of like in cartoons like when a lightening bolt hits. It sort of felt like that. I had a little internal monologue saying, "I think you're in love," like my subconscious had to spell it out to me because I wasn't getting the message. So I remember it was very exciting. It was like a lightening bolt, followed by little birds and I realized I had to tell the person right away.

—*Gwen*

Yes, I fell in love with his eyes. They were the color of the sky. I just couldn't stop thinking about them from morning until night.

—Sky Eyes Woman

I have fallen in love. Most recently with my current boyfriend. I think it took us a while. After we met it took us a while to start dating, and once we were dating it took us a while to get to the point where we felt like we were in love. It was just a slow realization of I would rather be with him than be doing things on my own. I would rather be sharing my space and time. I had always hung on to my personal space a lot. I was just happier to be in our space together.

—Caroline

Okay, I fell in love in the moment my children were born. It was one of those instant things.

—Hip Teacher

I have five great loves. There is a knowing that comes over you. The most dramatic and undeniable need to be close with your lover. Then there is another kind of drive that happens when your child is born and your entire being is connected to your baby. Both loves grow with time and last forever.

—My Mom

Yes, but I can't remember a process. It just happens like a whoosh and, after the whirlwind, it suddenly all makes sense, as if I've known my love my whole life and was bound to find him.

—Gina

It's different each time. One time it's a meteorite that hits you over the head and you wake up and there you are. Another time it's a very gradual process of peeling layers like an onion. You have an onion and there it is, and then you start peeling away layers and you get to places you hadn't really anticipated when you started. You're surprised and that surprise is good. And it keeps you off balance, that's the thing about love it's not about balance. You can't control love. You can work with it, you can approach it, and you can be in it, but you can't control it.

—*Eleven-Minute Love Man*

I think I explore every relationship with the expectation of finding love. I think you can love on all different levels. The process for me . . . it has always begun with a combination of feelings: attraction, respect, passion, shared values, or goals. When I make a connection like that, I begin to love parts of someone. If love blossoms, I search for the rest of the little puzzle. The rest is revealed in a physical connection. Electricity! I have found love many times, but there is another love, I think. I painfully push myself to retain morsels of hope for the great mythical love—a fantasy of my soul mate. When that process begins I think it will feel like a higher power. I believe that the type of electricity I will feel will fill me up so that every fiber of my body will know what to do.

—*My Younger Sister*

Well, I'm going to be fifty in two months. Love can be very different in different stages of your life. Love when I was young was really about self-discovery through your reflection on the other person. Now . . . I don't know . . . love seems to be more rational than passionate. It's still passionate, but the romanticism takes second place to reason.

—*European Man*

I've fallen in love once and actually that love was with someone who passed away in the World Trade Center. It was a hard blow in my life, because all of a sudden I didn't have any closure and it just left me pining for not being able to say goodbye. So it's just like a kind of never-ending struggle to try to understand what love is all about.

—*Dutch Gay Man*

Things happen; you talk, and you hold hands for the first time, then you go out, get drunk, and piss on each other. Then it's downhill from there.

—*Ejaculation Man*

When I was in the presence of this teacher in India I loved everybody. That is my ideal falling in love—like marrying the world instead of just a wife.

—*Love Force Man*

I really don't know. I've never been in love before. That's all I can say. I'm not an expert at this; you're asking the wrong guy. Listen, you'd be better off just selling me the flower. How much is the flower?

—*Sell Me the Flower Boy*

The sense of loss I felt when I left my fiancé behind in Chicago, along with my brother's illness, pushed me even harder to pursue my love research. However, before I could research love, I needed to figure out what love actually was.

LOVE RESEARCH HOMEWORK:
Have you ever fallen in love? Describe the process in your own words.

"Love is a mystery
in a mystery."
—*Vincent van Gogh*

Love Is a Score of Zero

The period before my love research began was a tough time for me. I was a stranger in a strange city, and my fiancé was hundreds of miles away. During quiet times I worried about my brother. I was lost and alone. Through habit I tried to find solace in books. But, it wasn't Charlotte or Emily Brontë that saved me. This time it was Daniel Webster who came to my rescue. Throughout my life, whenever I have questions and find myself at an impasse, I take my dictionary off the shelf and flip it open to find the answer or answers I'm looking for. Usually, when I've found a word's entry my search stops, and I accept its existence wholeheartedly. My confusion lifts as I gratefully read the word's pronunciation, etymology, meaning, and uses, all laid out on the page, carefully researched by the tome's tireless editorial crew. In confusing moments, a dictionary can be a meditative refuge where the whole universe from A-to-Z is bound together in a contained, manageable, alphabetically ordered volume.

What's in a Word

The dictionary had always provided me with hard proof of the reality and meaning of things, so it made sense that, when I felt bewildered by love, I would go straight to the Webster's Dictionary for answers. I skimmed past *lost*, *lottery*, and *lotus* and came to the L-word in question. The entry was medium length, longer than the entries for *lout* and *lounge lizard*, but more pithy than *lose* and *low*. There were eight separate definitions with multifarious meanings: A beloved person, warm attachment, benevolent concern, adoration of God, enthusiasm, devotion, the sexual embrace, and a score of zero. I read the definitions with interest, but for the first time, I didn't feel satisfied.

Exist \ig-zist\ vi {L *exsistere* to come into being} 1 a: to have real being whether material or spiritual <do unicorns exist?>
—Webster's Dictionary

When thinking about my brother, I realized that, even though language allows us to communicate ideas, express feelings, and exchange information, the notion of having common ground is misleading because it fails to take into account the individual variation that exists in language. Just as no two people have had the same experiences, no one's definition of a word is quite the same. In the case of love, its various meanings reside in the *minds* and *hearts* of all of us individually, and these personal definitions are not set in stone.

Rather, they shift and change with every life experience. I began to understand that my brother's definition of love had altered because his experience of reality had changed. His doubt set the word *love* into motion for me. No longer was it fixed in my mind like a word printed on a page. Suddenly it took flight and soared out of reach.

My family had shared a personal definition of love, it was a word we commonly used, spoke at the end of every telephone call, signed our names with, and often said in greeting and parting.

> Meaning does not truly reside within the word but in the minds of those who read it.
> —Webster's Dictionary

Now our communication was strained because my brother's illness had eroded the bridge of common understanding that connected him to others. The doubt that surfaced was also amplified by the fact that "love" is complex, maybe one of the most complicated words in the human language.

Let Me Count the Ways

Another reason for my confusion about L-O-V-E was the fact that, in the American English language, the word *love* is overused. Diane Ackerman writes in her book *The Natural History of Love*, "We use the word love in such a sloppy way that it can mean almost nothing or absolutely everything." In the United States, love is used so casually that it can cheapen, even negate the meaning of the word. *Love* is a commonly used verb that we use expansively to describe an incredibly wide-ranging spectrum of feelings.

In one memorable interview in Prospect Park, an African American actor with a commanding voice answered the question, **What do you love?** by listing everything in the world that he loved, stretching the uses of that little L-word to its limit. He smiled and laughed. I held the microphone up to his mouth and he began to speak, letting loose the wild flow of words, places, foods, music, people, and ideas that he loved. He flowed like a tap that was turned on. My arm ached holding the microphone up to his mouth to catch each drop. He just opened his mouth and all that he loved came gushing out, each word leading to another word alive and growing.

"... I love baseball; jazz; rock-n-roll; a sunny day; Prospect Park; *The Honeymooners*; football; my mother; my father, who I just met again recently; my brother who is no longer with us, but who is hopefully looking down and hearing this interview. I could probably fall in love with the person holding

> "I am so small I can barely be seen. How can this great love be inside me?"
> —*Rumi*

this microphone if I got to know her. Let's see, what else, oh chocolate milk! I love truth. I love comic books. Malibu—I love Malibu! Great place to hang out. I love the mountains in New Paltz. I love Bruce Lee films. I love Aretha Franklin. If I was on an island give me Aretha Franklin records and I'll be happy . . ."

He seemed to have no concept of time and I wondered if I should stop him, but the words kept flowing, so I decided I would not. He also didn't seem concerned that he may have gone over the two minutes I allotted to this question.

"I love vanilla ice cream, Swiss almond vanilla ice cream. I love reading the *New York Times* on a Sunday. I love school kids. I love education. I love my best friend, Ben. I love really, really good lovemaking. I love lovemaking that is not so great—still, *it's lovemaking* . . . I love my grandmother and grandfather, may their souls rest forever more. I love long walks in the rain . . ."

I wondered if he would ever stop or if I had just opened a Pandora's box that I would never be able to close because there are just too many beautiful things in this world to love.

"I love New Orleans, oh there you go, I could go on for another twenty minutes about New Orleans. I love the music, the people, the food—amazing place. It's completely out of control—anything that is out of control I tend to like a lot. I love Love. Love is a great thing."

Suddenly our eyes met and he stopped. There was a moment of silence filled with relief and triumph. I handed him a flower. Eleven minutes had just passed. Listening to this man in the park speak about all the things he loved made me question what "Love" really is even more so than before. How can we use the word *love* to talk about our feelings for both a city and our family, our favorite foods and the love of our life? I decided to do some more research, both on my bookshelf and on the streets to see if I could come up with an answer.

LOVE RESEARCH HOMEWORK:
Ask someone, What do you love?

Like Eskimos and Snow

We don't have an adequate vocabulary to fully describe our emotions. Love itself is universal, yet how people express the emotion to one another and how the word itself is used in language varies so much from culture to culture. There are some 6,800 known languages spoken in the 200 countries of the world. Imagine, then, how many different words for love exist. *Liebe* in German, *amour* in French, *liefde* in Dutch, *milosc* in Polish, *thanda* in Zulu just to name a few.

The way feelings are expressed in words also differs greatly from one language to another. In Arabic, *hubb* means love, but there are different words to describe the different levels and depths of one's love. In Spanish, there are also many words to describe different aspects of love that we English-speakers collapse into just one word. *Amor* expresses romantic love, *amistad* means friendship, and simple enthusiasm for something is *aficion*, so feelings can be described more precisely.

In many places in the world, the word *love* is almost sacred and is never spoken about. For example, "love" is not used so casually in Ireland. When I speak to my family on the telephone we casually say "I love you" every time we say goodbye, but in my experience with Irish friends and family this expression is not for daily use. Your actions themselves are meant to convey this emotion, so the word itself is not often expressed out loud.

In Japan as well, people rarely say "I love you" or *Kimi o ai shiteru*. A Japanese artist friend told me, "In Japan we do have the word "love," *ai*, but people don't talk about it much. We think the other person should know how much we love them by our actions; we don't have to talk about love because it's a feeling not just a word." When she first came to the United States she was struck by how expressing love verbally is so important.

"In America, if you don't say 'I love you' to a person, they might not know how you feel, while in Japan we don't say it, we have to feel it. American people always have to say, 'I love you, I love you, I love you' all the time. But I don't know how much they really love me. They use it so casually, almost like saying hello."

LOVE RESEARCH HOMEWORK:
Practice giving and receiving.

Taking It to the Streets

I decided I would attempt to find a common definition of love by gathering empirical data. I was armed with a new question in my Love Research deck, **What is love? Define it in ten words or less.** Some people gave short and sweet answers. Others rambled on and on in an impossible struggle to put their feelings into words. What follows is a collection of notable definitions gathered from New York City's streets. This dictionary presents a wide range of perspectives on love from people with varied backgrounds and cultures. I was struck by the contrasts in people's answers. They give you momentary flashes into the vastness of the word and a glimpse into love's manifold meanings.

L l

Love \ lŭv \ *n* ME, fr. OE *lufu;* akin to OHG *luba* love, OE *lêof* dear, L *lubêre*, *libêre* to please] (bef. 12c)

1 a (1): strong affection for another arising out of kinship or personal ties <maternal ~ for a child> **(2):** attraction based on sexual desire: affection and tenderness felt by lovers **(3):** affection based on admiration, benevolence, or common interests < ~ for his old schoolmates> **b:** an assurance of love <give her my ~> **2:** warm attachment, enthusiasm, or devotion < ~of the sea> **3 a:** the object of attachment, devotion, or admiration <baseball was his first ~> **b:** a beloved person: DARLING—often used as a term of endearment **4 a:** unselfishly loyal and benevolent concern for the good of another: **(1):** the fatherly concern of God for man **(2):** brotherly concern for others **b:** a person's adoration of God **5:** a god or personification of love **6:** an amorous episode: LOVE AFFAIR **7:** the sexual embrace: COPULATION **8:** a score of zero (as in tennis) **9:** *cap, Christian Science:* GOD—at love: holding one's opponent scoreless in tennis <won three games at *love*>—in love: inspired by affection.

Source: Webster's Dictionary

Trying to understand what another person needs and how to give it to them.

—Dying Partner Man

How you feel about people. What you think. How your body reacts and stuff like that.

—African American Seven-Year-Old Brother

Love is complete contentment and knowing I'll never be alone.

—Gina

Love is creating a universe with others.

—Art Educator

Love can be a lot of things on the inside, a sparkle, a twitter, a jump, a spin, and waves. That's five. Butterflies, whir w-h-i-r, briars, what kind of clouds are the puffy clouds? Nimbus clouds or cumulus? Cumulus clouds. I guess that counts as two . . . bubbles.

—Rachel

Love is what you think of in the dark.

—Mike

Honesty, no apologies; it's soft, it's forgiving, it's hot, it's exciting.

—Carousel Woman

I think love is the essence of the universe.

—*Karen*

No bullshit. Period.

—*Big Man*

I'm a lawyer and I can't do anything in ten words or less . . . hmm. Making a decision not benefiting oneself.

—*Sunset Lawyer*

Love is when you get something in return by giving nothing.

—*Family Man*

You know, poets have written epics about this, and I have to do it in ten words or less? Love is real. That's it.

—*Michael*

Love is the interaction of emotional necessity and physical needs.

—*Flowers Make Me Think of Death Man*

Plato wrote how many pages about love in the *Symposium*? This isn't a fair question. Well, this might not be pithy enough. Love should be an active and ultimately conscious expression of one's true self.

—*Ruth*

Love is Bear, my husband. He's big, and we're like a bear family. He's the Daddy bear, and I'm the Mama bear, and daughter was the Grizzly bear. Should have been the Baby bear, but she was so bad she got the name Grizzly bear.

—*Valentine's Day Woman*

Cultures have general definitions of what love is, but then we have personal definitions. We can go to a dictionary and look up the term and say these are the various definitions. It might be interesting to recognize there is more than one definition, so that brings into play what exactly is it? Having been a philosophy major and having studied language, I have a feeling that there are problems with words themselves. The more definitions we have for a word, the more we have to sync-up knowledge to experience a whole broad, integrated understanding of what love means and is.

—*Asian New Age Woman*

Love is the force that makes stardust tingle. The world is full of love but the distribution around the world changes.

—*My Mom*

Love is the only thing that you're born with that stays with you. And it's the only thing that matters in every situation.

—*Fourth Woman*

If you had nothing else (in the world) it would still be enough.

—*Young Woman*

Define Love in ten words or less. That's absolutely impossible. (Laughs)

—*French Miracle Woman*

I love you.

—*Three-Year-Old Kai*

Like care for each other, helping out each other, and like making babies, and living together and marrying each other.

—*Little Boy Who Wanted a Rose*

Getting married and having sex.

—*Little Boy's Friend*

Just the feeling when you see a special someone and they emanate energy. I've learned a great deal from the yoga community's research into energy exchange. I think love has a lot to do with how we magnetize each other. How we become attracted to people has to do with our magnetic fields. The total energy our being emanates. But then when you go even further there's the beauty of the soul, of the individual. . . . Each and every one of us in the park, in the world, we are all connected spiritually. We all have the gift of loving each other. We are all unique diamonds in ourselves. Love is the most beautiful connection that we are here to experience.

—*Asian New Age Woman*

Validating another's goals and dreams and life.

—*Music Woman*

Deep concern, passion, and joy.

—*Ian*

Unconditional expressions and thoughts of kindness, compassion, sharing, and gentleness.

—*My Elder Sister*

Love is never having to say you're sorry.

—*Superman*

Love is blue light dancing to a red bird's song.

—*My Dad*

Love is giving. Love is sacrifice. Love is joy. Love is pain. And love is great.

—*I Kiss the Ground Woman*

Love for me is communication, trust, commitment, and fun. If you can laugh a lot, it's probably close to love.

—*Married Man Woman*

Just ten words to describe love. Oh God. So many songs have been written about this. This is the most popular song. When you care about someone more than you care about yourself. When the knotted feeling in the stomach comes, the fact that the person is an extension of you, they're a part of you. What more can I say? I'm not eloquent enough to think of stronger objective words to describe love. It's too difficult.

—*E-Mail Love Man*

It's a feeling of being right about someone, a feeling of being wrapped up, safe, supported, and made whole.

—*Squashed as a Kid Man*

Overwhelmingly awesome. Outrageous. Beautiful. Soft. Sweet. Really difficult (laughs). Juicy. Raw. That would be it.

—*Juicy Raw Woman*

Love is patient. Love is kind. Love adores. Love is not jealous or envious. And love is everlasting.

—*Teen Christian Girl*

Love is a generous feeling that is unconditional.

—*Long Eyelashes Woman*

LOVE RESEARCH HOMEWORK:
Define love in your
own words.

_____

_____

_____

_____

_____

_____

_____

_____

_____

_____

_____

_____

_____

_____

Sharing, caring, selflessness,
adaptability, accommodation,
assimilation, progress, joint
effort, cooperative economics,
stability, intervention, growth,
humanitarianism, effort,
structuralism, potential
inventiveness, insight.

—Collaborator Woman

A kiss containing all of time with
no beginning and no end.

—My Younger Sister

Love is a glowing on the inside.

—Glowing on the Inside Girl

Love is when you give to give
and not to receive.

—Tina Turner Woman

Love is something I can use a
little more of.

—Little Girl

Visiting Hour

With all the countless definitions of love out there, my brother still couldn't find his definition or even believe that love of any kind existed. After he was diagnosed, he spent a few nights in the hospital, where my sister and I visited him. Down the hall there was a row of dark rooms. "The lights are out and I don't see him," I said. The nurse told us, "He's in there. You can go in and visit him now, it's visiting hour." My younger sister and I stood at the door, hesitant to enter because he had covered his body with a sheet. Standing there, afraid to enter my brother's hospital room, I wanted to live in a world with more love, where no one is ever a stranger because you see the whole world as your family, where every person around you is a parent or sibling, daughter or son. And more than anything else, I wanted my brother to believe in love again. Even if his definition was different from all the people I talked to on the street, I still wanted him to believe that love was real and that it existed in the world.

> *Omnia vincit amor.*
> (Love conquers all.)
> —*Virgil*

Me: Honey, we're here to visit you.

He didn't speak or move. So we pulled the sheets down from his face. I ached because it seemed like he wanted to hide from the world.

Me: Can we give you a hug?
My Brother: No, it's time for you to go.
Me: We just came and we're here to visit you.
My Brother: It's time for you to go.
Me: I brought you a picture of our family to keep you company. Can I leave it for you?
My Brother: No.
Me: I have a book about the solar system for you.
My Brother: No, I don't want anything.

I tried to imagine what he was experiencing. I knew he was feeling a profound sense of loneliness that was too much for his body to hold. He obviously needed to communicate, but something was stopping him. He seemed trapped in his own solitude, almost ready to burst from the internal pressure. I wondered what he was thinking about. Was he simply focused internally, noticing the beating of his own heart, the passing of blood and air through his body?

> "Love is the only sane and satisfactory answer to the problem of human existence."
> —*Erich Fromm*

Seeing him so resistant and unable to connect was heartbreaking, but it planted a seed of longing from which my love research continued to grow.

LOVE RESEARCH HOMEWORK:
Have you ever been without enough love?
Try abstaining from touch for one week.
Write about this.

Have you ever been
without enough love

The Greatest Love of All

A few years after my first Love Research interview, I felt as though I was only scratching the surface. As I collected more interviews, the project gained a little notoriety and I received an invitation from a gallery in Tampa to participate in a love-themed group show, *With Love from NY*, featuring New York–based artists. It was Friday when I arrived in Florida for the exhibition. The plan was to set up my Love Research station for the gallery opening that night, but I decided to spend my afternoon on the street doing interviews. A local artist I was staying with suggested I try the downtown center, and I set up across from a church that was staging a recreation of the crucifixion in remembrance of Good Friday. I had never seen anything like it before. A large group of Christians gathered in the church courtyard to nail a man dressed as Christ to the cross. It was a dramatic but disturbing backdrop for love research. I hoped that some of the crowd would wander over to my booth when the passion play ended.

Surely they would have some interesting things to say about love, since Jesus is, after all, a role model for love—one of the ultimate "love heroes." It's surprising to think that after so many hundreds of years, we have evolved so little in terms of our potential to love one another, but Jesus used to preach about the familiar issues of service and humility, the forgiveness of sin, faith, turning the other cheek, and unconditional love—as radical a concept today as it was in A.D. 33. Jesus's concept of love was a major historical breakthrough because he encouraged people to expand their hearts to love their neighbors and enemies as well as their family and friends.

An African American woman passing out religious pamphlets approached me. It seemed that we had both chosen the same location to find recruits. She wanted to be interviewed, so I asked her, **Where did you see love today?** She told me she saw love on the streets, when she was passing out "Tracks" to tell people about Jesus. I asked her if she loved herself. She replied, "I hope so. I wasn't born this way. I had self-loathing until I met God. He taught me how to love, so now I do love myself enough to love others too. Amen." I asked her, **Do you think love is increasing or decreasing in the world?** She seemed disheartened and said it was probably decreasing. "There's more evil in the world and, according to the Bible, times are going to get harder. It says love will grow cold at the end time, so I believe that is happening now." As she spoke, I felt a chill. I changed the topic and asked her, **How does one prepare for love?** She said, "I think basically you have to love your neighbor as yourself. The two commandments in the Bible are to love God with all your heart and to love your neighbor as yourself. That's how I would think you'd prepare." She looked at me neighborly and offered instructions, "Practice that. You have to learn these words and humble yourself and God will do the rest." I thanked her and handed her a rose. She neatly tucked it under her arm as she wandered over to the church where the passion play was ending. Luckily, one of the parishioners caught sight of my booth and headed over in my direction.

A stern elder African American man looked thoughtfully at my Love Research station trying to decide exactly what kind of mischief I was up to. He seemed slightly suspicious and had no interest in standing too close. I asked him if he would like to be interviewed. He shrugged his shoulders and said, "I will answer one question for you." I smiled and held

> "A new commandment I give to you, that you love one another, even as I have loved you, that you also love one another. By this all men will know that you are my disciples, if you have love for one another."
>
> —John 13:34–35, King James Bible

up a card. He read it out loud, **What do you love? List what you love in two minutes.** He looked at me and said, "Love is God, and God is love, so he's always with me. Is that good?" He seemed to have summed up everything he believed with that simple, straightforward answer. We smiled at each other and he moved on.

A young girl who had been silently watching off to the side stepped up. She was a dark-haired loner carrying a thick messy journal. I gave her the card, **Is love increasing or decreasing in the world?** She said abruptly, "I think people are becoming more and more selfish every day. This is going to be the disaster of society. So that's why I think it's decreasing." She was an unusually intense preteen, and reminded me of myself at that age. She took the next question, **Do you think you have the potential to love more deeply? What would that require?** "It requires great effort," she said with wisdom beyond her years. "Loving deeply is self-sacrificing and really knowing the other person and loving them fully and accepting who they are. It takes a lot of effort, constant effort, but it is the most wonderful thing in the whole world if you do it." How did she know this, I wondered to myself as I flipped the deck a third time. **What is your current relationship to love?** She said, "I've recently lost love, and I already have love, and I'm always looking for love. Well, I love a lot of people, and I love them very, very deeply, and when they go out of my life for some reason it's really devastating for me. I'm always looking for new people to love and share myself with. Every time you learn about a new person, you learn more about the world, more about humanity, and you learn more about yourself also. I like learning about other humans. Loving them is a way to learn about them. I'm always looking for love. I love to love people." I handed her a rose, and she opened up her journal so I could admire a freshly inked self-portrait she had made.

I stayed for several hours after the Good Friday service ended and watched as Tampa's sidewalk traffic trickled. It was nothing like New York. People just didn't walk around that much, nor was there any street culture. My booth was like a deserted island, devoid of street musicians, vendors, and people hanging about. I finally decided it was time to return to the gallery to interview a different sort of crowd.

LOVE RESEARCH HOMEWORK:
Stop and listen to street musicians. If you feel moved, make a donation.

I Got It Bad and That Ain't Good

A young rockabilly couple were the first volunteers. They approached me coolly, hand-in-hand. They wanted to be interviewed together. The man was handsome and assured. He looked over the question

What is love? (Define it in ten words or less.) "Okay," he smiled, answering in a syrupy Southern voice, "love is an instinctive trait, no matter if you have four legs or two, everyone is born with it. . . . I think love is the center of all life, it connects it together. If it weren't for the compassion that we feel for each other, that simple bond that connects everybody, in some sort of unconscious way throughout life, I think the whole world would fall apart." His sexy punk-rock girlfriend liked his answer and slipped her hand around the microphone to put in her two cents. "Love to me is waking up in someone's arms, the softness you feel, the glow. It's looking at someone and feeling like you are going to burst inside." She turned her head to stare at him as she spoke, "Your mind just goes blank. You just feel and that's it really, my mind goes blank."

I pulled out another card and asked them both, **Have you ever been without enough love?** He was taken aback and said he always had enough from his family, and for himself. She, with some discomfort, told me, "I think I felt like I was without love when I was younger because my mother was not around. I just hated life at the time and felt neglected. I felt alone for years. I think that's why I am so needy now." She laughed awkwardly and squeezed her boyfriend's hand. We ended our conversation with the question, **What is the biggest risk you have ever taken for love?** He let out a liquid laugh, "Oh Lord, that's a hard one. When people talk about risks for love, like in the movies, they are talking about throwing yourself in front of a car to save a baby, or giving a kidney to someone or something like that." He cleared his throat before continuing to speak, "If you think how amazing love is or how easy it is to get it, or how easy it is to give it—I don't think it's a risk at all. If anything, it's a profitable thing. Just the simple reward of realizing that Love is Free is a Hell of a reward in itself. And then realizing you can give it to somebody. I don't think there is any risk in love. I don't think I have had to take a risk. I think it's something that's been worth it every time I gave it."

The rockabilly couple wandered away into the gallery hand in hand. Most of the videos, installations, and paintings in the show, like mine, were filled with a longing for intimate connections in a city that is crowded, impersonal, and anonymous. A smiling middle-aged woman came toward me with a purple-haired teenager in tow. At first I thought they were mother and daughter, but then I realized the woman was the teen's teacher. They had come to the art opening together, which I thought was unusual and quite sweet. They obviously greatly admired one another and were comfortable in each other's company. The first question I asked was, **Who are your love heroes? Who taught you love?** The teacher laughed and said, "I think my biggest love hero is Cher. . . . When I think of Cher, I think of a giant red heart trimmed with black lace with 'I love you' written all across it. Besides, I love all that Bob Mackie stuff she has."

I asked the teen, **How does one prepare for love?** She patted her purple hair, and said, "I have to make sure I spike my hair . . . right." The teen held the microphone in front of her teacher awaiting her answer, "Well, I think one prepares for love by putting on a face. So I think if you are gonna get really serious about L-O-V-E, you need to do your eyes right and I think black eyeliner is definitely what you need for love." I handed them both a flower, and they asked me to take their photograph together, so I happily snapped a shot.

A young couple drunk on the cheap gallery wine stood and watched me for a few moments as I rearranged my flowers and checked my sound equipment. When I finished, they offered to be interviewed. I asked them, **How does one prepare for love?** She said, "One doesn't prepare for love, one hopes love will fall into your lap as many times as possible." He gave her the eye and said, "The best love catches you off guard and knocks you over," wobbling against her a bit then holding her shoulder to regain his balance. I asked them, **Have you ever fallen in love? Describe the process.** She smiled and said, "Yes, several times and it's like being reborn

> Human nature was originally one and we were a whole, and the desire and pursuit of the whole is called love.
>
> —*Plato*

every time. It's finding yourself—a security within yourself that you can't find alone. It's a completeness." He liked the sound of that and stroked her arm as he spoke, "The process is you see somebody and you think about them a lot. There's a connection and sometimes you have dirty fantasies about them, but that's just between you and me." He gave me a wink. I handed them a final card, **Do you think love is increasing or decreasing in the world?** He put his arm around her waist and said, "Definitely increasing. Women all over the world are becoming more free. So they are more free to love." He turned to face her when he said, "Yeah there's more love, that's why the world is getting so crazy. I'm serious. I think it will all end in one Big Love Explosion." And with that final sentence, the two shared a secret smile and left the gallery opening in a hurry.

Thinking about the teacher and student and the young couples I met in the gallery versus the seniors I met on the street, I started to wonder if people begin to think differently about love as they get older. Will the way I think about love when I'm seventy be different from the way I think about love now?

LOVE RESEARCH HOMEWORK:
Hold hands.

Wisdom from My Elders

You get the feeling that, along with almost everything else, love was simpler back in the day. People tended to marry younger and stay together longer. Societal attitudes toward sex have also altered the path of romantic relationships. One very generous elderly gentleman tried to pinpoint for me why it was so different back then, "I was young, twenty-two, and in a romantic relationship. I was in love before we did the sexual act—and then the sexual part came and it was a new powerful experience for me, more powerful than anything I had ever experienced, and it made my feelings stronger. The sexual urgency I felt transformed into a new sense of falling in love. I'm seventy and I think that it was different when my wife and I were young. Sex was less casual and available. I think romance was more a part of long-term relationships."

Of course, back then romantic affairs were still complex and difficult, and perhaps they always will be. But I think if we turned to our elders more often for advice on matters of the heart perhaps we would be less apt to repeat the same mistakes.

Our youth-worshipping culture often sees *Love* as a land populated by the young. The media rarely portrays romances about the elderly population or presents their point of view. In fact, once we hit retirement age the idea of romance is usually tossed out the bedroom window. However, over the years, people's views on love have changed so much that getting a perspective from someone from a different generation can be illuminating. Many of the people I interviewed said their grandmothers taught them about love. One woman shared her grandmother's rough and ready words of wisdom with me, "My love hero has to be my grandmother. She used to say, 'Don't be down with the maggots—always be on top of the garbage pile!' That meant, don't be wallowing with the maggots doing nasty things." Another wistful woman told me, "My grandmother who helped raise me, taught me a lot about love. She taught me love by sacrifice, and commitment to people, and also through work. She worked really hard for others, and in her work, there was love." Hearing my own grandmother's story of her no-nonsense romance during the depression always makes me smile, and puts my love problems in perspective. It was tough for them, they didn't have any money and, in her words, "they just scooted along." After years of "going together," my grandfather finally said, "let's get married." My grandmother accepted and the following Saturday they were married by the Justice of the Peace for exactly $2.00. It wasn't a fancy start, but they were happily married for over forty years.

While I was doing my love research, I went home for a summer holiday and visited my grandmother. Several years ago we had almost lost her, so this visit was urgent. After nearly a century of loving, my grandmother is our family expert. All of us turn to her when we have unanswered questions, and I wanted to interview her.

Here are my grandmother's answers to my questions on love:

🦢 How does one prepare for love?

You don't prepare for it. It just comes to you. Naturally.

🦢 Do you love yourself?

Oh sure, I have to love myself! Otherwise how is anybody else going to love me?

🦢 Do you think you have the potential to love more deeply?

Oh I really don't know. I think I love all my children, my son and my daughter and grandchildren. I don't know if I could love more deeply because I already love as deep as I can go I think.

🦢 Who are your love heroes? Who taught you love?

My whole family. Nobody taught me, you get to know it and it's in your heart. There isn't anybody around that I really hate. I love 'em all. They're all very good to me. My children, my grandchildren, I just love it when they come to see me and I get a hug and a kiss. I look forward to letters. I never write any letters. You should see the terrible writing I have. So if I call on the telephone that's about it. And my grandson comes to see me every Tuesday and we play cribbage. He's teaching me how to play cribbage and I like that, I like that.

🐚 Have you ever fallen in love? Describe the process.

Well, I fell in love with my husband. First of all, I had seen him a few times and he had a car. I used to talk to him over the doorway, you know? I wasn't supposed to go anywhere and when I stood on the sideboard and stuck my head in the car window he rode away with me to the corner. Then, over five years, we got to be really good friends. The first year I wasn't allowed to go out at all. He couldn't come over even to visit me. I used to meet him on the corner by the church, but then finally he got close enough to my mother that she allowed him to come to the house. We started going out together after that. Then we decided we had waited long enough and were going to get married. We didn't have more than one paycheck between us, but we got married on September 1, 1934. We were married forty-three years before he had a heart attack and passed away. He was eating a peanut butter sandwich and all of a sudden I heard boom, and he was on the floor. That was hard to take (voice cracks in tears). But it was a good way to pass away, you know without being ill. But it's still hard on the family.

🐚 Have you ever been without enough love?

I could always use more love. I always can. Whenever I see any of my grandkids I just squeeze the dickens out of you. I love you all. So that's what I can say. There's not enough; I take all I can get, every bit of it. How about a kiss? Seal it with a kiss.

I was so grateful that my grandmother and the elderly people I met on the streets took the time to tell me about their views on and experiences with love. After listening to their nostalgic recollections, I began to consider my experiences of love from my youth. How would I tell my own story to my grandchildren someday?

LOVE RESEARCH HOMEWORK:
Ask your elders about their love experiences.
Record their answers for posterity.

All I Have to Do Is Dream

For the young, love is often a one-sided affair, with romance existing only in the imagination. One wary teen I met told me, "I've never fallen in love. I've had crushes though." First crushes are rarely consummated, and sometimes teens don't even have the courage to tell each other how they feel. Friends often have to play a part in the saga. At thirteen, you get tapped on the shoulder and someone whispers, "He likes you, he told me to tell you." Or your messenger might help you by passing your note to the boy in the first row. For a group of young boys that I interviewed, courtship itself seemed like playacting, at seven they were already well versed in the dating game. I asked them, **How does one prepare for love?** and the first boy answered, "Ask if they want to go on a date and take 'em out to eat or something like that. Then ask them where they live and can you have their number and help them out." And his friend responded similarly, "You take people on dates and take them to your house. Take them places to get clothes, jewelry, stuff for their house, protection, old sneakers, cars, stuff like that."

All those years before you make physical contact with another human being you might spend hours daydreaming, just building up to that moment. Maybe you practiced kissing techniques in the mirror. Or wrote romantic scripts of all the things you would like to say. Wouldn't it be great if the more you daydreamed about love when you were young, the more time you received now, for the real thing?

When I was a teenager I spent a lot of time daydreaming. But for that I needed solitude—something hard to come by in our crowded house—so I found my retreat in books. I took one with me everywhere I went, like a friend. Opening the cover, I slid in, to wander alone through the limitless realm of my imagination. And it was from books that I first learned about romantic love.

All of my first loves were characters in books. Teenage boys just didn't measure up to Heathcliff, Rochester, or even Holden Caulfield. In my inexperienced mind, romances were complicated dramas cast full of dreamers pining for unrequited love. I was always attracted to the dark, brooding poetic types whose contained passion made them alluring but explosive. In these stormy love affairs there were always obstacles to surmount, and struggles to overcome, before the lovers could come together, face-to-face, in the end. Desire was drawn out for ages of agony before the triumphant girl could finally meet her match and get that passionate kiss on the moor. Of course the romances were only imagined, but I cast myself as the heroine of each story I read.

I was a late bloomer, and embarrassingly so. At seventeen I was full of self-doubt because I had never been kissed. At that insecure age, physical love was important because it showed the world that you were approved of and desired by the opposite sex. But a kiss could also be dangerous because for a moment you opened up your own private world to another, giving them, as poet John O'Donohue says, "absolute permission to come into the deepest temple of your spirit." As a teen, I yearned for acceptance but also saw myself as a bit of the outsider. I read a lot of poetry and agonized that I might end up a lonely old bird like Emily Dickinson. I felt past my prime, like a sad, long-forgotten carton of milk with an expired drink-by date. Boys had held my hand and taken me on dates, and even given me admiring pecks on the cheek, but no one had ever given me what I craved: a full-on open-mouthed French kiss.

I craved a mouth-to-mouth meeting with someone intelligent, intense, and poetic. Since I was romantic, I often preferred living in my imagination to reality. I fantasized all the time about kissing or being kissed. Actually that might have been the crux of the problem, because like a lot of teenagers these days,

> "I feel this pang inside—is it my soul trying to break out, or the world's soul trying to break in?"
> —*Rabindranath Tagore*

I was stuck in virtual reality. I would lie on my back on my parents' bed holding my mom's silver hand mirror up to my face to catch a glimpse of what my lover-to-be would see. I practiced sultry gazing.

I finally got my chance for a fairy-tale kiss when I got an Italian American boyfriend who had the best name, Dominic Vacca. He wasn't a poet, but he was a citywide soccer star and seemed comfortable in his athletic frame. I knew he would know just how our lips should finally meet. One night I stepped out onto our front porch to say goodbye to him and he held me around the waist. Then he came in closer until our lips touched. Our mouths parted, and met, slowly, like the doors of our souls opening. Then, I felt an unexpected and forceful intruder: *his tongue*. I panicked. I had pictured this moment for so long and breathlessly waited for the fireworks to start. Unfortunately, despite his good looks and great name, Dominic hadn't yet mastered the art of kissing. But it didn't matter. I had finally had my first kiss!

We said goodnight and I danced up the front steps of my house feeling ten times lighter because I had been initiated and set free from the curse of solitary confinement. Dominic was my first kiss, but not a great one. But the door had cracked open, and love would finally be able to enter. Once the door to physical love opened, the reality of what love really was started to finally shine through.

LOVE RESEARCH HOMEWORK:
Test the effect of different kisses on the body.

A Lifelong Romance

No matter where I interview people, self-love seems to play a crucial role in everyone's ability to love and connect with other people. "If you're not in love with yourself, no one else is going to be," said an inspiring African American woman who stayed with me for the weekend, a union organizer visiting from Minnesota who had eleven children and fourteen grandchildren. On the streets of New York City the same assertion came up: unconditional love for another is only possible when a person genuinely loves him- or herself. Most described the process of falling in love as a dramatic self-transformation, akin to losing one's mind or being reborn. Their sense of self was actually altered when they merged with their lover, as the "I" became the "we" both emotionally and physically. Without a strong sense of individual worth and selfhood, interviewees said it would be nearly impossible to develop a lasting and healthy relationship.

Elizabeth Kübler-Ross, a groundbreaking Swiss psychiatrist, called "unconditional love"—the love we have for others and the love we have for ourselves—the ultimate lesson that we all have to learn in life. If love is the definitive lesson that we are here to learn, then it seems to me that American society as a whole is not structured to foster this growth.

LOVE RESEARCH HOMEWORK:
Skinny-dip.

Love Thyself

What is self-love? Is it the act of recognizing your failures and successes, your strengths and weaknesses and accepting them? Is it looking at yourself in the mirror and smiling at what you see? How does our American culture measure a person's value?

Unfortunately, Americans often measure men and women by their accomplishments, especially in terms of economics. Too often a person's worth is measured by the amount of money they have in the bank, the objects they have, or the clothing they wear on their body. "We run after values that, at death, become zero," says Kübler-Ross. In America's competitive and individualistic society it's difficult to achieve self-love because we're constantly comparing ourselves to others and finding that we don't quite measure up. After all, how can you give yourself value in a country that doesn't value the qualities that you hold? This may explain the cultural mania for self-improvement:

the obsession for therapy, weight-loss programs, and exercise. Thomas Merton said, "What can we gain by sailing to the moon if we are not able to cross the abyss that separates us from ourselves?" There is simply no replacement for self-love. If you don't love yourself, you'll be continually searching for someone else's acceptance. You won't see the possibilities right in front of you. In her seminal book *All About Love*, bell hooks says, "Self-love is the foundation of our loving practice. Without it our other efforts to love fail. Giving ourselves love, we provide our inner being with the opportunity to have the unconditional love we may have always longed to receive from someone else." You can only allow someone else to love you to the extent that you love yourself. And it's equally true that you can only love and accept another person to the extent that you love and accept yourself. If you can't love yourself, you'll have a difficult time loving anyone, and you'll resent the time and energy you give to another person that you aren't giving to yourself. In poet John O'Donohue's words, "The more love you give away, the more love you will have." So take the time to love the people around you and watch how the love you have for yourself grows as well.

> " If we truly know and understand that we have a limited time on earth—and that we have no way of knowing when our time is up, we will then begin to live each day to the fullest, as if it was the only one we had. "
> —*Elizabeth Kübler Ross*

street dictionary

∂℧ Do you love yourself?

Girl, yes, I love myself. If I don't love myself, who else is going to love me? I love myself because I have to put clothes on my body. I have to wash my body. I have to go out and do things. I have to say *"Self, I'm okay even though you're a little overweight."* I'm working on that; I don't have to feel bad about the way I look. . . . Sometimes you look in the mirror in the morning and say, "Uhhh," but then you get it together, brush your teeth, and hair, put a little makeup on. . . . If you're not in love with yourself, no one else is going to be.

—*Deb Howse*

Yo me quiero. I love everybody, Mami.

—*Mami Lady*

I do love myself. I suppose my parents taught me how to. They always taught me I was the best thing. They always called me Sugar Pie and Sweetie and Dumpling. I knew they meant it 'cause I was sweet and sugary and everything good that there was.

—*Sugar Pie*

Well, Oscar Wilde says, "To love yourself is the beginning of a lifelong romance," and I always liked that. I do think I love myself, not all the time, of course. I think I've always felt this growing up in a really loving house. My parents' enormous love for me makes me love myself. I never have thought about not loving myself. I guess I never thought there would be another way.

—*Ian*

Why not? I am the best person in this country.

—*Bullfighter Man*

I hope so. I wasn't born this way. I had probably self-loathing until I met God. He taught me how to love, so now I do love myself enough to love others. Amen.

—*Amen Man*

I do love myself, and because I love myself I am trying to overcome my complexes. I'm a Taurus, and Venus—the planet of love and beauty—rules me. I have a lot of love to give.

—*Glittery Eyelids Girl*

I would say I love myself very much. If I can't love myself, I can't love anything. I was taught to love by my grandmother, mother, and father. You know, they always tell me, "Brenda I love you" before I go to sleep, so it taught me how to love other people.

—*Girl Basketball Player*

I was kinda born this way. Yeah, I love myself. I got really good parents when I was adopted.

—*Five-Year-Old Kira*

I love myself but in a nonpossessive kind of way. I love the spirit that I think is in myself, the spirit of life. I had to learn how to love; it is a long process. A lifelong process in my opinion.

—*Twin Poles Man*

I'm growing to love myself more and more. I went to California, and my friends were really into their self-help stuff, and I think it's a way to love themselves. So that was nice because you can love yourself easier in California. I do sometimes get down and think I am entirely useless, but I feel like it's going to be an amazing summer.

—*Housekeeper Lover Man*

I guess I love myself because it seems if you didn't love yourself you wouldn't have a reason to live. You have to. It's sort of egotistical, of course, because, you know, sometimes you go, "I'm pretty today," or there are some points when you go, "I'm dumb, I'm dumb, I'm dumb." But you still like yourself anyway.

—*Enemy in Books Girl*

I was born loving myself. I definitely was. I was a very cheerful child, very content and very together. Sometime in high school I started falling apart, and I'm just starting to put it together again. Most days I feel really self-critical. I think being self-critical is incompatible with self-love.

—*Egg Woman*

I'm sort of a misanthrope, and it comes from not being so in love with myself. So I'd say no. I don't think I was born this way. It's something that has happened over time.

—*Misanthrope Man*

That's an extremely difficult question to answer. I think it's funny because I've begun to love myself less and less since moving to New York. I think that when I was in my teens up to around twenty or so, I felt like I loved myself and accepted myself. Now that I am here I feel very blah. You know what I mean? Love is a very active emotion, and I feel very blah right now, which is not very active. I don't hate myself, and I don't think I'm doing something wrong. But I just feel very blah right now.

—*Blah Man*

It's been a struggle, but I love myself now. I just think that, growing up, maybe I never felt good enough or I had really high standards of what I should be. When I was twenty I would think by the time I am twenty-five I need to have achieved this or that in terms of artistic success because I am an artist. It was kind of hard. I could feel myself start to panic when nothing happened to me like that. Now that I've just kept working I just feel better about it. I've kind of accepted things.

—*Man #2*

LOVE RESEARCH HOMEWORK:

Do you love yourself? What about yourself do you love? Don't be modest. Make a list and be specific. Keep it at hand when you feel a bout of self-doubt or when low self-esteem creeps in. While you're in the mood, make a list of the things you love about your friends, family, and loved ones. Send them a copy in the mail.

_____

_____

_____

_____

_____

_____

I had to learn how to love myself. It took awhile. I think I started loving myself when I was fourteen. All my family members were very negative towards me. So when I reached that age and started interacting with others, and noticed that boys started liking me, I asked myself what do they like? I looked in the mirror, picked what I liked about myself, and started loving me.

—*Caribbean Woman*

The Stranger in the Mirror

Where does our ability to love ourselves come from? Is it something we are innately born with, or is it something we must learn? I remember fragments of psychoanalytic theory from my studies in graduate school that shed a glimmer of light on that question. A mother's love is the first thing we know, but the first primal experience of love is one-sided. Newborns are receivers of love. They haven't yet learned how to give back that love; it's something we learn over time.

When we're born our mothers provide for all our needs—their bodies actually give us the sustenance we needed to survive. A new mother provides her baby with everything; she gives it food and drink and provides for all its comforts. There's hardly a separation between the child and the mother—they are one.

When you're young, you don't love yourself; rather, everything you touch and experience becomes part of you. You see yourself in everything: the sunshine, your mother, the sky. As newborns, we don't understand that we are separate and mortal. A sense of selfhood has not yet developed. I asked people to go back to their earliest memories and tell me about their personal love development. Their answers were revealing. Many learned how to love from their parents and families, but a great many grew up without enough love in their lives. Most admitted that they were still trying to overcome that lack.

street dictionary

Were you born loving yourself or did you have to learn how?

I had to learn to love myself because I was born here, but when my mom and dad were going through a divorce I moved to Trinidad. Then I came back and went to school in Manhattan. I was the darkest person in the class and I had an accent, a weird accent they had never heard of, you know. So I used to get teased and made fun of, and I would try to fit in. I tried to hide my accent and hide other things about myself that would reveal I had another culture. So I did have to learn to love myself.

—*Unprotected Sex Girl*

Yes, I love myself. I believe that when my mom passed away it was a very rough time in my life so I didn't love anybody. But I'm regrouping, and it's very hard; well, it wasn't so hard; it was more like I had been broken. I can never be broken again because the damage has been done. When something is broken into so many pieces, you know, there's always cracks, even though they're glued together. The cracks are still there and the pain is still there, but it subsides just enough for you to make it through the day. People don't realize what they have until they lose it.

—*Drugged Woman*

I think I have finally gotten to the point that I do love myself. I don't think I was allowed to love myself when I was younger. It wasn't until I was in my thirties that I discovered some of the ways I was squashed as a kid and not allowed to express or feel anything—either happy or sad. All my feelings were bad, so it was hard to love myself. When I look at pictures of myself as a child I look sad, depressed even. I look like I have the world on my shoulders. So it took a long time, and a big part of that was finding the right woman to love. I have been with a lot of different people and it was always disastrous, but then I met Barbara. Because of some of the work she has done in learning how to love herself, she has really enabled me to see I could love myself too.

—*Squashed as a Kid Man*

I had to learn how to because I had tough times. Lots of people didn't love me, so I didn't love myself. Then, once I gave them the boot, I started loving myself.

—*Previous Lives Woman*

I have this strange concept of self where I don't believe there is a you and a me. Why look at the individual self when there is the meta-self, which includes everything I can look at? If I know through experience that nothing I'm feeling, nothing I'm thinking is separate from the meta-self, then that is everything. Then I know I am one little brain cell, one little synapse, and one little subatomic particle in the cosmos. Do I love myself? Yeah, I love myself.

—*Hostage Man*

I never get to a point where I am a hundred percent satisfied with myself, because it drives me to go out and achieve more. There is something about feeling just enough dissatisfaction with the self that can be productive at times. I have read a lot of psychoanalytic theory, and, according to these theories, we are born not so much loving ourselves as thinking that the whole world is us. We don't differentiate between others and ourselves. So everything is there for us, and everything is part of us. I believe that it is a huge loss when we find out the whole world doesn't exist for our pleasure and our parents are not there to simply provide whatever we are hungry for on command. That is the moment self-love kind of ends simply because the self has become really delimited.

—*Homay*

I don't think I love myself. I think I like what I've become and what I'm trying to achieve every day. I like the person I'm trying to be. I try to keep improving and becoming the person I'd like to look up to or to resemble, the people that inspire me. That's a process that is something you work on every day, becoming who you want to be.

—*Rapture Man*

Ahh!! (laughs) I think if I didn't love myself I would not have really loved life. You know, I think that is where the power is. I don't boast about loving myself. I just know that it's there because of how I treat life and everything around me.

—*Gentle Man*

When You're Smiling
(The Whole World Smiles with You)

As you can see, learning to love yourself is often not something that happens overnight. This was the case with my brother; it took him a long time to accept himself. After years of stifling his emotions due to his illness, I remember when my brother started smiling again. It was something so simple, but unimaginably precious. His healing began when he took steps to learn how to love himself unconditionally. He made a daily commitment to recovery by accepting and appreciating the life he had been given, regardless of all the difficulties he faced. Gandhi said, "My imperfections and failures are as much a blessing from God as my successes and my talents and I lay them both at his feet." That is exactly what my brother did.

LOVE RESEARCH HOMEWORK:
Buy an outrageous mirror. Smile at your own face every day.

After many years of being unable to accept his diagnosis, he finally met with a doctor to get medical treatment for his illness. When he finally found acceptance, it was a struggle to find the right medicine to help him. Each drug had to be tested with painstaking trial and error to see how it affected his body. He also tried many different approaches to healing: drugs, exercise, meditation, and creative expression all helped him regain his inner balance. The process was slow and tackled day by day, with many emotional and spiritual struggles along the way. It took infinite patience and incredible inner discipline.

My brother's fate could have been different. Living in New York City, I see homeless men and women every day. It agonizes me because I know many of them are mentally ill. In fact, Roseanne Haggerty, the founder of Common Ground, an organization with a mission to end homelessness, said in a recent lecture that 30 percent of the adult homeless population suffers from some form of severe and persistent mental illness. If our society were based on love, things would have to be different. In a better world, we would never allow anyone to spend even one night sleeping on the streets because everyone would be treated as someone who was loved.

I truly believe that the love in my brother's life made his recovery possible. His good health is the result of my family's love and deep commitment to one another. Without daily nurturing, this kind of

> "Don't look for miracles. You are the miracle."
>
> —*Henry Miller*

healing would never have been possible. Also, for me, my brother's recovery was the ultimate testament *to* love. His commitment to himself is a pure expression of self-love that is an inspiration to everyone who knows him.

I've looked to my brother for the courage to face a difficult situation many times and, through his years of personal struggle, he has attained a deep inner peace, a resilient approach to life, and a gentle spirit. Being in his company is always easy because he has a rare unconditional acceptance for himself and every person around him. Throughout my research, my brother has stood on the sidelines cheering me on, "Celebrate and enjoy life sister! In general things may be in disarray and turmoil but all people are intrinsically good—if you believe that—keep doing love research."

Over the years I've realized more and more how much my brother and my family mean to me. When asked what I love best, they are always one of the first things that I list. On a typical day, are you surrounded by the things that you love? Or do you find yourself separated from the people, places, and things that are most dear to you?

LOVE RESEARCH HOMEWORK:
Collect love songs. Broadcast your favorite song into the street.

Stop! In the Name of Love

I wondered to myself, is there a way to see love every day? A way to appreciate life and glory in the present moment more fully? As I inched my way into my thirties, my girlfriends began calling me with their agonies over love. My poetic Iranian American friend told me one frustrating day that she had an epiphany. She woke up and thought to herself "maybe life is my lover." Instead of ceaselessly searching for *someone* she decided to do things differently. From that day on she vowed to embrace her life, making every moment count by spending a little extra time with people. She started appreciating all the loving people in her life, like her landlady who was like a mother to her. She embraced her roommate every day when she came home from work. She appreciated the small exchanges she had with people on the street. She adopted a more loving attitude, and people reflected that back to her. She asked her coworker one day why she was smiling at her and the woman said simply, "Because, I love you."

I noticed that the days that I ran the Love Research station were different from the rest. Dressed in my red suit and hat I approached the world with more warmth and love. People on the street were, in turn, more open to me. Strangers started stopping me for help. Tourists asked me for directions when they never had before. People started conversations with me and were drawn in almost magnetically. Something had shifted energetically, like a switch turned on. There was a striking contrast between my working days and Love Research days. When I was a passenger on the subway traveling into Manhattan for my day job, no one ever talked to me. Weekdays I was sealed off from the city, connection was impossible. I almost *repelled* strangers. But on the weekends when I set up my Love Research station, I was an open circuit, and people flowed to me.

The question, **What do you love?** always had a mysterious effect on people. During some interviews, people channeled what they loved stream-of-consciousness, like a magical incantation. Caught in waves of memory, recalling every moment they had been touched by love, some people found it difficult to stop speaking. It seemed as if, by speaking, they were releasing a little bit of their love out into the world.

J. L. Austin, the British philosopher of language, came up with the interesting idea that speech itself

> Love is the great intangible.
> —*Diane Ackerman*

is a form of action. In his influential book *How to Do Things with Words*, he defined a form of speech called "performative utterances," which are sentences that don't just *say* something, but rather perform a certain kind of action. Sentences like "I do," as uttered in the course of a marriage ceremony; "I name this ship the *Love Boat*," in a dedication ceremony; or "I give and bequeath my watch to my brother," as occurring in a will all take action and make something actually happen in real time. I would suggest that naming what we love is also a kind of performative utterance. When we name what we love, we actually make something happen. What we love becomes charged with our energy. We activate a relationship and, by doing so, we create a new kind of existence for it. When we list all the things in our life that we love, we learn something about ourselves by the relationships between those things, and also become aware of all that has not been named.

🐚 **What do you love?**

I love girls 'n' motorbikes.

—*Biker Man*

I love men. I love food, I love to drive a car, I love sexy clothes, I love nice flowers (ones that smell good), I love people, I love to be an activist, I love talking to people, I love old people. . . . I love to travel, I love to get my nails and feet done when I can afford it, I love to buy sexy underwear, I love to do backrubs for people, I love to make people at peace, cook sometimes, I love to take a nice refreshing bath and just chill out . . .

—*Deb Howse*

Ahh, I love my partner, and I love all the things about him. I love how he smells in bed. I love certain parts of his anatomy that I don't have to get into. I love music; nothing is so full of solace as having the right record at the right time. And I love our home; we've bought almost nothing, it's all things that friends have given us, or people who have died, some my grandmothers. It's all stuff we've collected in our lives and it's just so comfortable. It's fabulous! And I love our friends. I'm always astounded that they love us back, but again that's me.

—*Dying Partner Man*

Snowflakes. Sunshine. Fresh laundry. Getting lost in the woods. Running down to the lake in the middle of the day to jump in the water. Having blueberries by the edge of the lake. Having a midnight beach party. Building a fire. Calling my grandmother and my great-grandmother and talking to them in the morning, having them tell me about their lives. . . . Hearing Bach's *Mass in B Minor* with a huge choir all around with the voices swelling up is wonderful. It's also important when people come to negotiations and peace after being in war and there's not enough peace in the world. Also, when someone reaches out to you when you need it most.

—*Farzi*

My husband, my boys, my family, good health, nature, dirt, trees, sunshine, flowers, buds, all colors, fresh fruit and vegetables, the ocean, life, photographs, memories, connecting, inspiring, drawing, space, outside, fresh air, my friends, my pets, dance, music, wildness, expression, art, all art, learning, animals, travel, new ideas, insights, newness, wisdom, connection, warmth.

—*My Elder Sister*

Mama, papa, my brother, my grandmas and grandpa are so lovely, aunts, uncles, cousins, normal toys, trucks, chickens. I like my garden, I like clouds, kitties. I love them. I like trees, plants, grass, houses, paint, ladders, candy, flowers, gardens, Peter Rabbit. I love him.

—*Three-Year-Old Kai*

First of all I love my Lord, and then I love myself. It's deep. Seriously, I'm a master playboy and I love women. I love to make them—as well as myself—feel good. Sexually, if a woman don't orgasm before me I feel I haven't fulfilled my obligation. Don't get a misconception—if she don't orgasm—I'm not coming. It's best when the couple come together. Climax together, that's a beautiful feeling.

—*Master Playboy*

Cuban cigars, good scotch, the perfect golf shot, walking a golf course, boating, catching fish, flowers, that's what got me to come over to you.

—*Florida Family Man*

Women. I'm getting sad that we're coming into fall and the women are going to put on their long coats and I won't be able to see them in the raw. I love everything about women: eyes, hair, shape, form. Did I say enough or do you want me to go into more details. Specifics, okay. I love women. I mean it's like everything. It's the way they walk, it's the way they're shaped, it's the way they look, it's the way they cook; but you know, I can cook better than they can. I'm a good cook. What else? I love being alive. I'm always happy to wake up and be alive and get an extra day outta God.

—*Drunk Natalie Wood Man*

She: I love Rice Krispies. I love
Jimmy (laughs).

He: I love this woman . . . okay
as many things as we can . . .

She: Rainy days.

He: Snow.

She: Quiet peaceful time.

He: Shakespeare.

She: Clean sheets.

He: Solitude.

She: Music.

He: Mozart, roses, Cezanne.

She: Trees, fresh air . . . we don't
get enough of that lately.

He: Sundays and any days you
don't have to work.

She: Four o'clock in the morning
conversations.

He: Writing a poem, writing
anything, writing a love letter.

She: A nice long shower.

He: Even better a hot bath, beer.

She: A good haircut is good.

He: Yeah, a bad haircut is not
something you would love.
Just being alive.

She: I love the way Jimmy
smells.

He: Stop, this is getting way too
personal . . . her hair, her
eyes, her lips, her face, her
ears . . .

She: My pimples!

He: (laughs) Well, those I'm not
sure I love, actually.

She: Running water.

He: I love running water.

She: Just so relaxing.

He: A nice breeze, meeting
strangers doing love
research.

She: Yeah that's pretty
awesome.

He: With a huge vase of roses.

—Love Duo

Family, kisses and hugs,
animals (top five: kitties and
dogs, frogs, turtles, otters,
baby farm animals), plants
(top five: succulents, big old
trees, flowering trees blooming
in spring, herbs, vegetable
gardens), friends, memories,
laughing, hopes, daydreaming,
travel, chocolate, swimming,
salami, holding hands, beaches,
tide pools, forests, stars.

—*My Younger Sister*

I love Robert, my husband, and
our dog, Alfie, most of all. They
make me happy every day. I love
my family and the sound of my
little nieces' happy giggles when
I speak with them on the phone.
I love being secure and content,
safe and snug at home. I love
nature and the sea, the English
countryside, and long walks
along the coast.

—*Gina*

I love New York, I love dancing,
I love theater, I love what's
happening right now, I love the
stage, I love lights, I love music,
I love my family, I love my hair.
I just shaved my head (laughs
hysterically). I love my scalp.
I've always had long hair so
this is a totally new experience,
and I love it. . . . I love eyes
and looking at people's eyes.
I love people. I get a kick out of
people. I really do, and I love
watching people walk down the
street to see how they interact
with each other.

—*Bald Michelle*

Chocolate, any kind of
chocolate, cake, my boyfriend,
my son, space, silence. I love to
laugh, music, and the beach.

—*Wendy*

Survivor, *The OC*, *The Bachelor*. Let's see, can the things I love be people? Colin, my mom, my whole family, my sisters, my brother, and my nieces and nephews. Chocolate, marijuana, beer, and life and sunsets and clouds—pretty clouds I mean— my friends, flying, TV, New York (sort of), cooking.

—*Katrina*

He: Doggies, we love doggies.
She: Macaroni and cheese.
He: Beer.
She: You.
He: You.
She: My family, and painting.
He: Good books.
She: Vacations, the ocean.
He: Yeah, the ocean.
She: Warm socks.
He: Yeah, that's about it.

—*Married Couple*

In Russian, a little boy asks his grandmother, What do you love?

(She replies in Russian.)

He translates into English: She likes her grandson and granddaughter. She loves all her children. She likes this beautiful air. She loves animals. She likes flowers. She likes music. (He stops and asks her, What kind of music?)

(She answers in Russian.)

He translates into English: She likes classical music. She likes going to forests and jungles, and she likes picking up you know . . . mushrooms.

—*Russian Grandmother and Grandson*

My partner in life. I love that he is my best friend, confidant, and lover all in one. My family. Watching each amazing child grow. I love hearing them laugh together. I love listening to their ideas. I love that they share so much with us. I love the smell of the earth responding to a spring rain. I love watching green tips of growing plants poke through the dirt. I love poems by Mary Oliver, high billowing skies, flesh tones in different lights, flip-flops, skinny slices, green lemongrass tea, patios, yellow sunlight shining through leaves. I love shadows dancing on the fence, paintings and painting, grandchildren.

—*My Mom*

Time with my family. Travels with my amazing beautiful wife and, when possible, my great family. Warm Mediterranean beaches. Denmark and Ireland, India with friends. Reading books to my nephews, then acting the stories out with them. Enjoying my wife's ethnic cooking, the many recipes from my mom, or from the children's recipes. Music to set the mood, live or recorded, especially played or performed by family and friends. Art: poetry, artwork, writings, drawings, paintings, songs, stories, dances, theatre, from family members and friends. Love Research, for its honesty and sensitivity. Family memories and memorabilia, antiques, artwork. The smell of spring gardens, small fuzzy animals, fresh produce from my own gardens . . .

—*My Dad*

My wife, my father, my mother, my sister, my nieces (laughs). I love kimchee. Can I be as honest as I choose? I love art, I love to drink, I love sex, I love to masturbate, I love the city of New York, I love this piece, I love to teach. What do I love? That's a good question.

—*Art Curator*

Coffee, conversations, kissing is definitely on the list, movies. I love first dates (first and second dates usually), I love e-mails from people I haven't heard from in years. I love photographs, good rock 'n' roll. Poetry is up there. Books, quiet. I love the sunrise when I've been up all night (clears throat). I love . . . most of Bob Dylan's songs, women for sure as a whole are fantastic. My brother, my friends, and good whiskey.

—*Sexy Smoky-Voice Man*

I love the inside of a person. I prefer someone who is sensitive, so they could teach me. They could be there for me when I need it. And they make me feel real special.

—*Dominican Man*

I love myself, I love basketball, I love the world, I love some kinds of people but not all people, I love cleanliness, I love thoughtfulness, I love cars, I love money, I love *women*, I love some guys, my father, my cousins, my uncles, I love nature.

—*Lesbian Teen Basketball Player*

I love many things, but the greatest love I have right now is my Lord and Savior, Jesus Christ. That's the greatest love any man can possibly get or have.

—*Latin Believer*

Peace and quiet, pausing thoughts, no thoughts at all, my dog, the view out my apartment window, fall, comfortable shoes—which is funny, I don't have many—good hair days, coffee and cigarettes—those are big—the smell of flowers, my family, my sisters. I could cry answering these questions (chokes up). . . . Finding my nook in my boyfriend's arm. It's the best place on earth. Hugging my mom doesn't happen a lot, but knowing she means it and isn't doing it because I started it. Making people smile, kids, little babies, big fat faces, drums, heartbeats. What else? Knowing we just had an eclipse, knowing that a lot of people are looking at the same things at the same time—knowing we are all thinking the same thing. Rainy days, cigarettes, and coffee . . .

—*Coffee and Cigarettes Lover*

I love my ex-girlfriend, I love my family, I love the vast mystery of life, I love sunsets, I love light, I love coming out of my apartment in the morning and seeing the morning light illuminate the tops of the buildings. It is like this soft golden glow and that just really gets me going; that's wonderful. I completely love music and community and radical self-expression. Joyous celebration of life is really something I love, sharing in spontaneous creativity. I love screaming really loud if I have to, spinning around in circles really fast, whatever it takes to shake my foundations. I love sitting down at places that say Love Research and giving interviews because it makes me feel like I am living an interesting and exciting life.

—*Man Wearing Heart-Shaped Glasses*

LOVE RESEARCH HOMEWORK:

Close your eyes and take a deep breath. Dispel every thought that is distracting you: the laundry that needs to be done, the bills to be paid, the mile-long list of things to do. Let your mind be clear and present. Make yourself comfortable and relaxed and take two minutes to name everything you can that you love. Acknowledge everything in its particularity. Be as specific as possible. Free associate and follow your own stream of thought.

_____   _____

_____   _____

_____   _____

_____   _____

_____   _____

_____   _____

_____   _____

_____   _____

Has your love
ever been tested

Shot Through the Heart

A few years into my love research, the first weekend of October was still sunny and warm. The Lower Manhattan Cultural Council had invited me to conduct love research at their Culture Fest booth in Battery Park. I was setting up when I noticed a homeless woman begging for change at the entrance gates. Her face was dirty, her clothing bedraggled. She noticed me and wandered over to see what I was up to. I was horrified when she came closer; in the center of her forehead there was a deep, round hole. The opening must have been from a circular wound that healed on its own. From its shape and size, it could even have been a bullet hole. That seemed impossible: how could she have survived being shot squarely in the head? She certainly never went to the hospital, because a doctor would have stitched that wound shut. She also had many missing teeth, making it difficult to determine her age. She could have been anywhere between thirty and seventy.

She asked, "What are you doing?" And I answered, interviewing people about love. She laughed lightheartedly and said she wanted to be interviewed too. I silently handed her a card, **Where did you see love today?** She said, "Out here in the street from all the people giving me money." I handed her the next question, **What do you love?** Her face broke into a joyful jack-o'-lantern smile, "I love my husband, and I lived with him for fifteen years. I love my husband and my cat." I was surprised by her answer. Why was she alone now? Were her husband and cat roaming around the streets somewhere too? I asked her another question, **Do you love America?** She didn't hesitate, "Yes, I do because it is the land of the free." I was taken aback again. She was a homeless beggar in the streets, what exactly did she mean by land of the free? How could she be patriotic and still believe in the American dream? I tried to get her to elaborate by asking, **Has your love ever been tested?** but she gave an ambiguous answer, "Every day. I live with my boyfriend—it's tested by proving to him that I love him." Then I pulled out a final question, hoping it would shed some light. Reading the question out loud she said, **Have you ever been without enough love?** Her answer was stunningly simple: "No." She flashed a grateful smile, and held out her cup to me for an offering. When I handed her a rose instead, she accepted it with exquisite pleasure.

A matronly Eastern European woman in a tomato-red uniform with brass buttons arrived at my booth. She looked like a lost member of a military marching band, but the badge fastened to her lapel made it clear she was a security guard. Her accent was thick and sounded put on, almost comically so. I asked, **What is the biggest risk you have ever taken for love?** and she answered, "I zink the biggest risk is you have to realize is zhat you have to sacrifice certain zings like your time, your soul, your spirit." The next card read, **Do you think you have the potential to love more deeply?** She answered hypothetically, "Yes, zhat would require to spend more time together. To see what this person is inside. How interesting zhis person is. See if people have the same point of view or maybe different, and I zink that people should be on the same intellectual level otherwise one of those people vould get bored." In order to get her to reveal more I asked, **What do you love?** Her eyes danced all around the park naming whatever inspired her. "I love animals, I love nature, I love people, the whole vorld: birds, squirrels, and vhatever is alive I love it. I zink that it's very important to love all living zings because we need to learn how to survive together. We call it "symposium"—like the academic get-togethers of the Greeks—but not many people know how to survive with each other. We either love or we don't love, but regardless, we need to know how to communicate

> I am he that aches with love. Does the earth gravitate? Does not all matter, aching, attract all matter? So the body of me to all I meet or know.
> —*Walt Whitman*

with each other because that's very important." She gave me a jolly thank you for the rose and marched away.

A sad-eyed Latino man with a rolling voice appeared at my side. He sniffed the roses and said he wanted one too, so I asked him a question, **What is your current relationship to love?** He answered me passionately, "Right now I'm looking for love. I believe that the greatest love we ever have is to be in communion with Jesus Christ. That's the greatest love I have ever achieved or been with. I'm still looking for Mrs. Right. Who knows maybe someday I will find her or maybe I won't. But right now I'm content with my Lord and Savior, Jesus Christ." I asked him, **Have you ever been without enough love?** He looked forlorn and slowly answered, "Yes, I have. I believe loving someone and not getting the same love in return can be frustrating, but I have to be content that the love grew in my heart. You know, I have to be pleased with that. If I didn't get the love back I hoped at least I have to be happy it grew in my heart." I handed him another card, **Has your love ever been tested?**. He sighed and quietly spoke, "My love has been tested many times. One of the times it was tested my first wife caught me with someone else. I had to make a choice of whom I wanted to be with. She was testing me to see where my love stood. I failed the test because I wasn't honest with myself or with her. I cheated, I lied, I manipulated, and I wound up alone because of it." Finally, I asked him, **What do you love?** He named his dog, friends, and family, his car, and then he looked skyward, "I love many things, but the greatest love I have right now is my Lord and Savior, Jesus Christ. That's the greatest love any man can possibly get or have." He picked out a rose with careful determination to find just the right one and said, "God bless you," as he parted.

LOVE RESEARCH HOMEWORK:
Carry a sign that says, "Kiss Me."

Love-Starved

My family was camping together in the lush Pacific rainforest. Several years had passed, and my brother's health had returned. We felt grateful to be together. We joked like we were kids again, enjoying the easy weekend together. Everyone else had turned in for the night, and my brother and I were sitting at a dwindling campfire. The blackness surrounding us was vast, and we admired the sky together. Watching the stars led us into philosophical discussion. He asked me if I wanted to play a meditation game called *What If*. I agreed, so he told me the rules.

"The point is to imagine that something doesn't exist anymore. Taking turns back-and-forth, we name whatever comes to mind. I start and say, *No wood*. You say, *No fire*. I say *No banks*. You say, *No credit*. We keep going like we're playing ping-pong. Each word triggers another word. Let's try it. Ready?"

The firelight flickered as we stared into the flames.

No sister.	*No brother.*
No music.	*No dancing.*
No weapons.	*No war.*
No money.	*No shopping.*
No words.	*No books.*
No Facebook.	*No friends.*
No America.	*No states.*
No seeds.	*No trees.*
No teeth.	*No smile.*
No stars.	*No heaven.*
No religion.	*No God.*
No economy.	*No jobs.*
No time.	*No clocks.*
No love.	**No Love . . .**

My mind blew, like a fuse. Imagining a world without love overwhelmed my circuits.

"You win," I say. My brother says there aren't any winners or losers in this game, it's supposed to open your mind up. "I'm stuck though . . . my mind went blank," I said, "I think the game stops here."

Thinking about a world without love, I realized that, beyond tragedy, loss can also be a teacher. To develop understanding we can't take anything at face value, we have to look deeper. True knowledge is gained through direct experience. When you lose something—even temporarily—you begin to comprehend its value. For example, you lose your keys for an afternoon and suddenly they seem golden. When you find them again you hold them more tightly. In the case of love, you know it best when you're lonely and it seems out of reach. As they say, absence makes the heart grow fonder. That's also why the most powerful love songs in the world are filled with heartache. Nick Cave, the Australian rock star, says it best, "We all experience within us what the Portuguese call *saudade*, which translates as an inexplicable longing, an unnamed and enigmatic yearning of the soul, and it is this feeling that . . . is the breeding ground for . . . the sad song, the Love Song." In the middle of the night, if you've ever been alone, craving to be held, you know what love is. One man I spoke to told me about how he once desperately drove cross-country, all through the night, just to reach a friend. He needed to be held—he needed love—that badly.

LOVE RESEARCH HOMEWORK:
Hold someone.

street dictionary

🐚 Have you ever been without enough love?

Every day.

—Towers Woman

No!

—Three-Year-Old Kai

Ah no, Mami.

—Mami Lady

Yes, I spent pretty much most of my teenage years without enough love. I think only now since I love myself I am making up for some of that deficit.

—Short-Answer Man

I would have to say yes. I have been without enough love . . . um . . . having been in a marriage for almost six years, with a man who was, I believe incapable of showing love. He was quite capable of showing anger, showing rage, but not love, no, and I just felt terribly deprived of it. Love-starved, you might say.

—Softball Woman

I couldn't get enough love when I wasn't able to love myself. I do love myself now.

—Linda

Yeah, I worked in a job where I had to do body retrieval for a morgue. . . . It gets to a point where sometime you have to do such horrible things—a young girl in her twenties died and they didn't know why. I had to physically restrain her mother from even touching her. Then a friend of mine, the only other person in the city I knew, happened to die, and I had to handle his body the next day. Then there were a series of fires in the building where I lived. It was just building up to the point where I simply needed to be protected. So I got in my car, and I drove and showed up in New York. I crashed on people's couches, and a good friend of mine just slept with her arms around me—nothing sexual—and it was the best sleep of my life because I felt loved and protected, and it was something I needed.

—*Lost Man*

Yes, as a teenager.

—*Gina*

Yes, I have really learned that there is no such thing as having too much love to give, and I have also learned there is no such thing as receiving too much love. I have been without enough love in a way that has left me hungry on the streets and truly at risk for not continuing to live. I love being alive, and I love the fact that there is enough love for me now. I hope there is love for others who need it too.

—*Lesbian Mom*

I am an only child, so I think I had a lot of lonely times. My parents got divorced when I was young. I was five. So I feel like I had periods of time in my life when I was just sort of under the radar. I had to be really active to seek people out in some ways.

—*Long Eyelashes Woman*

There have been times when I thought I was unloved. . . . I remember being a teenager desperate for the feeling of love, feeling unrecognized and under-appreciated. And then, at some point, realizing that my parents were just so busy with nine children, that they just didn't have enough of themselves to go around. Well, that's where peers and sibs enter the stage. I believe adolescence is that special time when one begins to understand the joy of giving love as well as receiving it.

—*My Mom*

Definitely. As a child I did not have enough love, at least consistently from my family. That definitely affects who you are and who you become, which makes it even harder and more special when you love yourself again and find people that love you. I know love comes mostly from within, it doesn't have to come from family or someone around you.

—*Swept Off Your Feet Woman*

Yes, many times (laughs). I guess the question for me is what constitutes *enough* love? People don't love themselves enough, so it is very difficult to have enough to share with somebody else.

—*Professor Douglas*

On an objective level I should say totally not. God or a cosmic energy or whatever you want to call it loves you all the time. I think we are just so blessed for being alive that we should never feel like we've been without enough love. Yet we all, including me, feel that we are without enough love at times. I think that's just because we are blinded by our feelings and the false sense that we are alone when, in fact, there are all these beautiful people everywhere.

—*Handsome Gum-Chewing Man*

I think mostly what drives me is the lack of love in my childhood. I was born during the war and never really had any heroes. . . . I'm from Lebanon. The wars with Israel and other wars were tough. I never really experienced the stability of family.

—*War-Torn Teen*

Hell yeah! I think, growing up, I was without love constantly. Being without love, I don't think you realize it until you actually have love. I mean what's your point of reference? I think until you're really loved, you never have enough. There can always be more love in your life. But yeah, I think until I fell in love I was constantly without enough love, and it wasn't a sad thing because I didn't realize it. If you're blind and one day you have sight, you realize then, "Oh, that's the difference!"

—*Expensive Lingerie Woman*

Yes, of course—well, actually the first things that come to my mind are times in my life when I've felt that no one loved me. Probably every human being has gone through that, even if they can look at their lives objectively and say that's ridiculous. Everybody goes through some kind of moment like that. I think actually the times that I felt that I really was without enough love were when I was the one who hadn't been loving. So if you're without enough love, it's not so much that people don't love you enough, but it comes more from you not putting enough love out into the world.

—Ruth

Yes, I have learned that love is always available and is all around me. You can find it when you are open to it and believe that you deserve it. The only times I have been without enough love have been times when I have strayed from myself, not loved myself enough. I have gone though times when I have had to work hard to love myself more and I always find that every drop of love I give myself is magnified in the universe around me like a ripple in a pond.

—My Younger Sister

Yeah. That is an interesting place to be. You can either choose to be angry with the world, you can either think this is the permanent way the world has to be, or you can go out and see what you can do to change it so you have enough love. Everyone's choice is individual.

—Media Woman

Yes, right now. I wish I had that sense of feeling alive and vibrant with energy rushing through your veins at this very moment. I wish I had more of that. Having enough love has to do with loving yourself first. In this particular moment, yes, I think I am without enough love. And they say when you look for something, you can't find it. You shouldn't search, because it makes you desperate and because all that reaching and grasping isn't necessary. You should be healthy and grounded and always search for self-love first. Understand that's where it all starts from. There's definitely a way to start from within.

—*End of Love Woman*

Certainly I have felt a lack of love. It kind of closes your world in on you. You feel like a stranger to other people or a stranger to yourself. When I feel that is happening, I just kind of check in with what I know to be true. This reminds me of something else. I was going to bed one night and I was thinking, "Oh man, I'm kind of lonely, it would be nice if someone was here." I closed my eyes and this spring of emotion welled up inside me and it said, "You have an infinite resource of love within you, and you don't need anyone else to show you love." We are always searching outside ourselves for love or for calmness or peace, there is this constant worry to find it. I realized in that moment it was all inside me already, so I didn't have to worry about it and everything was okay.

—*Man Wearing Heart-Shaped Glasses*

As I thought about the question, *Have you ever been without enough love?*, I realized that I was lucky enough to have the love I needed, but how did I—and everyone around me—prepare for love?

LOVE RESEARCH HOMEWORK:
Have you ever been without enough love? Write about how that felt for you.

How Do You Prepare for Love?

Each Love Research day starts with a flower-buying mission. I head to the neighborhood market to purchase the freshest bouquet of roses I can lay my hands on. I always spend a long time making the selection. Roses are my lure. I've had to become a floral connoisseur, strategically picking the choicest blooms.

Roses have always been valued for their beauty and have a long history of being used as love symbols. The ancient Greeks and Romans identified the rose with their goddesses and called it the flower of love. There was even a language of flowers originating in Persia in the fifteenth century, which was later brought to Europe. In the nineteenth century, this floral code became popular, and people sent messages in bouquets to each other. Since each flower, color, and number had a specific meaning, conversations between lovers took place without a single word. Today, roses are just as popular and are still universally considered to be symbols of love. The flower industry is a booming business with the estimated annual global market at about $40 billion for cut flowers, dominated mostly by trade in roses.

Peering into the heart of each flower, I finger the circular rim of spreading petals to judge the condition of the bloom. I try to calculate just how long it will last. I sniff all the various scents, seeking the most pungent fragrance among them. Inspecting the rainbow of colors, I attempt to make a precise selection for the hue. I always choose flowers in a range from pale pink to a deep crimson, since red is the color that most often comes to mind when we think of passion, desire, and love. My roses usually sparked a little joy and I made sure they were bright and dazzling enough to stop even the busiest New Yorker in their tracks. Each choice is important to me because the flowers are my neon signs, sending a powerful message of love out into the streets.

Over the course of many years of researching love, I have spent a small personal fortune on roses. I have to attract people all day, so I always buy two dozen to make an eye-catching presentation. When I think back on all the smiles they brought to people's faces, I am certain that it was some of the best money I've ever spent. I spent a lot of time, money, and energy preparing for my love research, and I was very interested to learn about the different ways in which people prepared for love themselves. The answers were as beautifully varied as all the people I interviewed.

LOVE RESEARCH HOMEWORK:
Plant flowers.

street dictionary

🐍 How does one prepare for love?

Look the other way.
—Juicy Raw Woman

One breathes in deeply and exhales and opens wide.
—Inn Owner

Be love itself. You can't know love unless you are love.
—Open-Book Woman

A job, career, good education, and a car.
—Hope Boy

By being a gentleman. . . . By serving them their dinner (giggles). By pouring their champagne (giggles).
—Little Boy Who Loved the Sound of His Own Voice

I think basically you have to love your neighbor as yourself. Two commandments in the Bible are to love God with all your heart, and love your neighbor as yourself. Practice that. Learn it and humble yourself, and God will do the rest.
—African American Jesus Woman

Safe, safe, safe sex.
—Sanitation Worker

You make yourself into the person you would want to fall in love with.
—Visual Thing Woman

Calming all the voices in yourself. Opening your heart to whatever and whomever happens.

—*TV Talk Show Host*

When I am in a needy space . . . one of the best ways to open myself to love again is to put myself in a place of selflessness and kindness, to put myself in a place of compassion. If I look at the world from that place I find my needs decrease and my heart opens. That is when I find I am most prepared.

—*Fear Sells Man*

I don't think you ever can prepare for love. It's like a runaway train. It hits you and hits you hard. If you're lucky you'll get hit more than once in a lifetime.

—*Runaway Train Woman*

It involves the practice of love. There are things you can do to help manifest the love that's in you more freely. A couple examples would be: always think of God. Whatever God is to you, always keep that in mind. Another thing is working on developing your own character and being very tolerant and nonjudgmental about other people. Look at other people's faults—no matter how gross or offensive—not as your problems to fix or change. When you point the finger at someone else you have to remember there are three fingers pointing back at you. Whenever you are a critic and it involves a separation between you and me—that's the opposite of love. Love I find is a unifying force, it leads to a oneness.

—*Expansive Man*

Maybe the two lovers or the one who wishes to be a lover or a beloved can read Plato's *Symposium*. It's really good reading. I think it can teach anyone about love: the dynamics of it, if love is an example of how we exist, what forms we exist in, why it happens, and who it happens to and with.

—Plato Girl

I think a lot of heavy reading is involved, you know; you have to get yourself educated with the classics, and you have to listen to a lot of love songs and also read some pornography, and then you're ready.

—Rockabilly Man

We feel love from the very beginning. We're conceived and we get here by lovemaking. It is the first step to life . . . when a baby comes out everyone oohs and aahs over the baby. You get all kinds of people loving, kissing, hugging you. . . . When we grow up it's a different story. We don't get that much love from people. . . . My thing is if you can hug somebody, tell them to have a good day, if you can kiss them on the cheek or shake their hand, anything like that. I think we should, because we don't have enough contact. I will touch anybody from all walks of life.

—Deb Howse

Holy Smokes. I don't know, maybe you should go to a lot of psychotherapy and read about Buddhism and New Age spirituality. I don't think I am prepared for love. It's never enough and I never know how to get what I want. I always have a tendency to feel hurt, so I think in order to prepare for love you have to undo ego. You have to let go and let yourself be caught. And you can't really prepare for being caught.

—*Chocolate Girl*

I think people should be sent to school to be taught how to love. I think it should be the most important part of the curriculum. I think that you have to know how to be kind, know how to show your feelings, and know when someone is trying to show their feelings to you. What's the game of love? How to court. How to turn down a courtship. You think you know all these things on instincts?

—*Superman*

Earth Angel

When I set up my booth to research love, I became an unlikely source of inspiration in the city. "I was just coming home and I saw this wonderful lady with roses and I think that is what we need . . . a love research laboratory. That's what we need," a French mother enthused. My *Love Research* sign signaled like a beacon to everyone who passed by. The people that were drawn to me made me realize that love is not just a noun or an object to be sought. It's an active verb, an attitude, and a way of life. If you want love, you simply have to find a way to embody it. One woman put it quite succinctly, "You can't know love unless you are love." When you express the love within you, others will feel free to express their love as well. Suddenly, you'll be surrounded by it.

In many interviews, people told me that seeing my booth was a sign of love for them. A gentle African American man stood at my side for ten minutes watching me interview. After a while he told me in a soft voice that he was my guardian angel. I had always wished for a guardian angel in difficult moments, and his words were strangely comforting. When I asked him, **Where did you see love today?** He looked into my eyes tenderly and said, "Today I saw love right in front of me. Right here."

When I asked other people, **Where did you see love today?** some were momentarily stuck. Though it took some tough and harried New Yorkers a moment to readjust, almost all of them were able to stop and see everyday life through the lens of love. Their answers became expansive, "I saw love at basketball practice . . . in an amazing evening sky . . . in my children's eyes . . . in my mother's generosity . . ." When everyday perception is subtly shifted, love can be seen everywhere.

LOVE RESEARCH HOMEWORK:
Try reading Plato's *Symposium* and ask yourself, "How do I prepare for love?"

street dictionary

🐍 Where did you see love today?

At practice. I love the game so I practice really hard. I guess I have to really love it to stay because coaches was really killin' us today (laughs).
—*African American Teen Basketball Girl #2*

I saw love today in an amazing evening sky. It was just perfect like Christmas in the air.
—*Buddhist Man*

When I woke up (laughs) and I looked over to my right. That's where I saw love today.
—*Young Spike Lee*

From you. There's lots of love at grandpa and grandma's house.
—*Three-Year-Old Kai*

I just came from a memorial for a friend of mine who just died a month ago. She was like my hero, one of my spiritual heroes. Today we had a memorial at the Film Anthology Archives for two hours, and there was a lot of love.
—*Star Man*

Wherever I look there is love. Keep an open mind and just enjoy the beauty that life has to offer. That, to me, is love.
—*Latin Man*

I saw it in my cat—who always wants to be petted and talked to and noticed.
—*Russian Elder Woman*

I just saw love five minutes ago coming over the eastern side of Union Square. A large group of young people appeared who were the cast of *Hair*. They wore retro sixties outfits, and carried tambourines, drums, and a large banner that said "Aquarius Love." They were singing. It just made me really happy, as they had this great energy about them. So I hung up my cell phone to get in on that love because it looked like it was going to feel really good. So we danced around and we sang and it was really joyous; they gave me flowers and it made me happy.

—*Man Wearing Heart-Shaped Glasses*

In my wife, her smile and her body. My children's photos, their art, their voices on the phone. In the poetry of life. The sun, the blue sky.

—*My Dad*

I see it in a lot of people loving one another. I feel like everyone out here in Gay Pride could give each other a mass hug. That's how I feel—like everyone's in a demonstrative mood. It's really nice.

—*Jovial Puerto Rican Man*

Sitting in the garden in the spring sunshine with my boys.

—*Gina*

In a couple of friends. Celeste and her husband, Joe. Every time I see them together there's something indescribable between them. You can tell they don't even have to talk to one another. Just being next to each other, you can tell by their body language that they really love each other.

—*Connecticut Man*

I saw it in my children's eyes.

—*Mother and Son*

I watched a mother holding a child, her cheek against the silky hair, her nose behind the tiny ear. She looked drunk with love.

—*Linda*

Right there (points to her son and kisses his head).

—*French Mother*

Anytime I see attention. I see love connected to anything with attention. When someone is concentrating or caring for things in a certain way. Those people who are meditating in the park over there now. They are doing a loving action. I see the tree branches moving; to me, that's divine love just wafting through the breeze. Something is much greater than us and is taking loving care of us. All that love just goes into everything we see.

—*Expansive Man*

My three-year-old ran upstairs to wake our five-month-old from his nap. I could hear him soothing him on the baby monitor. I found them snuggling and laughing together. My husband took them on an expedition downtown to ride the monorail. Goodbye kisses from them all. I watched my husband leave with our baby boy in a carrier on his chest, our older son on his shoulders. Later, I sat looking out the window. I saw a pair of crows gathering sticks together to create a nest.

—*My Elder Sister*

I think from the moment I got up I've been seeing love. From the moment I opened my eyes and my cat was standing next to me with that look as if to say, *Good Morning, Mother, I'm glad you're awake, it's time to eat.*

—*Softball Woman*

In a take-away box from Toteros Restaurant: ravioli, gnocchi, and meatballs all wrapped up in memories and slowly cooked red sauce, A bottle of sand from the beaches in Alabama, the smell of my pillows, a plate of cookies, conversation with my mom (making dates to have lunch, and plans for Europe), my nephews, this research and its author, my brother's kind heart, Jessie.

—*My Younger Sister*

At the Love Research center. I walked by and thought what a wonderful idea. Love, probably the most important thing in life, is something we really don't pay that much attention to in regards to really understanding what motivates ourselves to act and to live. So I saw love today in Love Research. Thank you.

—*Sixteenth Man*

Just down the street, I ran into some friends who were passing out flyers for Gay Pride. . . . They both asked about my partner who is in the hospital right now; he's probably dying. It's really tough, a very difficult situation. That kind of love has been given to me in the past few months that he has been there, where almost every day he has died, but he is still hanging in there. For a really frail guy, whose character is tough, but whose body has never been, I feel that his survival is a kind of love for me, and definitely what all our friends have given us. That's love.

—*Dying Partner Man*

It's easy to see that love is all around us; all you have to do is open your eyes. There are also many ways to prepare for love, but it occurred to me that preparing for marriage—a commitment to life-long love—was different in some ways.

LOVE RESEARCH HOMEWORK:
Paint a room red. Remind yourself that love is all around you.

From This Moment On

How do you prepare to love someone for the rest of your life? The question was never far from my mind as I neared my wedding day. Marriage preparations in the United States usually focus on the trappings of love, hurling the bride-to-be into a desperate Bridezilla hunt to find all the necessary fixings for wedding "perfection." With so much bridal shopping, there is often little time left for deeper contemplation about what a lifelong commitment actually *means*. Since I was so far away from my husband-to-be, the nuptial details seemed somehow less important and almost trivial. Neither of us had ever put too much importance on the signifiers of love, and besides that, we were broke artists.

Before I moved to New York, we had a giant rummage sale at which we sold most of our possessions. Our yard was filled with secondhand wicker furniture, stacks of books, cooking pots, and the record collection I inherited from my father. We watched as every discarded item was snatched up like a treasure found. The thriftiness of the sale made me almost gleeful, and we raised just enough money to purchase two plain gold wedding rings for $75 each at a store in Chicago's historic diamond district. I liked the simplicity and sameness of our gold bands—and the fact that they were imbued with only the personal significance we gave them.

Most men these days save up to buy their fiancé a proper diamond engagement ring, but I have never been much for diamonds. During the Depression, my grandfather gave my grandmother a cigar band to wear on her finger as a promise ring, and it took years until he could actually afford a diamond. As a teenager, that story represented "pure romance" to me, and it made a lasting impression. My grandparents, parents, and in-laws-to-be had all been together for forty years or more, so I knew loving for life wasn't an act to be taken lightly. I also knew that a wedding ring was just a starting place, a symbolic circle on your finger to remember the commitment you made.

Love's a Verb

Why is it that, as a nation, we have not yet realized our true potential to love? It may be because our capitalistic society is not based on a loving ethic. Capitalism is a highly individualized, product-driven system that reduces everything—even love—down to terms of economic value. One man I interviewed said falling in love was like shopping, "You don't know what you're looking for, but when you find it, you'll know." But if shopping for love is the metaphor we live by, it also suggests that if you're not satisfied with the person you're married to, it's easy to replace him or her with a better model. In fact, America has one of the highest divorce rates in the world, with "40 or possibly even 50 percent of marriages ending in divorce," according to *Americans for Divorce Reform*.

Falling in love in our culture is also often presented as a matter of chance, something that happens *to* you. Romance in television and the movies usually only shows the beginning of love—the just-smitten stage—then abruptly cuts to a happy ending, as if a couple's story ends there. But love is not often shown as an action that you need to make happen every day. These misconceptions are largely responsible for much unhappiness and the disintegration of many relationships. Like many people I interviewed, I once believed love was largely out of my control. Our bodies operate on automatic systems—

we breathe, our blood circulates, and our hearts beat without any conscious effort—and I assumed that love worked effortlessly in the same way. But, "love is most often defined as a noun, yet . . . we would all love better if we used it as a verb," writes bell hooks. Love Research made me see love as an active force that we *make happen* every day. We are all responsible for creating it.

Guided by Love

What would a world actually look like if love were the guiding force? I believe a society ruled by love would have to be structured in a radically different way. People would no longer be driven by the need to have more, but by the desire to live more fully, making the most of what they have. What if spending time with the people you love took precedence over everything else? The way we spend our time every day would have to be adjusted.

I did an online search to see if I could find statistics on how average Americans spend their time and found some interesting results. The amount of time people spend loving is insignificant compared to the amount of time they spend doing other daily activities. The U.S. Bureau of Labor Statistics' recent *American Time Use Survey* found that employed Americans (between the age of twenty-five and fifty-four) spend 8.7 hours working, 7.6 hours sleeping, 2.6 hours engaged in leisure sports, 1.1 hours eating and drinking, 1.1 hours doing household activities, 1.7 doing other activities, and only 1.2 hours caring for others in an average day. Over the course of a lifetime, this means you spend roughly twenty-three years sleeping, nearly twenty years working, ten years in recreation, over six years eating and drinking, and around six years caring for others. When I looked for more detail, there seemed to be little research available on how much time Americans spend engaged in loving acts, but I did manage to find one interesting statistic on AmusingFacts.com that says that the average amount of time spent kissing in an entire lifetime is 20,160 minutes. That is 336 hours of lip locking, or fourteen days of kissing bliss. When I sum it up like that, my mind immediately imagines the possibility of taking in all that kissing at once in a two-week mouth-to-mouth marathon.

" Be the change you want to see in the world. "

—*Gandhi*

Why not add up how your daily hours are spent, and see how you really spend your time? Looking at my own Time Use Survey, I found my days to be seriously lacking in time spent loving. I have vowed to give myself gifts of time. I am going to pledge more minutes spent for loving, more moments for caring for my loved ones, and more time for caring for myself. How can I prepare to love my husband-to-be for the rest of my life? I love each and every day as consciously and actively as I can and will continue to do so throughout our marriage.

LOVE RESEARCH HOMEWORK:
For one week find out how you spend each day. Add up the hours. Could you be spending more time loving?

Going to the Chapel

According to the U.S. Census, 2.2 million marriages take place in the United States every year. That breaks down to more than 6,000 wedding bells ringing in just one day. On a brisk, sunny November day, my husband and I added our names to the count. The extra-long Thanksgiving holiday gave us the perfect weekend to get hitched; thanks to the Office of the City Clerk it was amazingly easy and affordable. New York requires a twenty-four-hour waiting period between getting a marriage license and exchanging vows. We obtained our license on Friday afternoon ($35) and married on Monday morning ($25), leaving the weekend in between for my husband to get more familiar with the city.

The simple ceremony was not overly romantic or spiritual, but it swiftly did the deed. We were in and out of the chapel in less than two minutes and left the building holding hands as husband and wife. On the sidewalk, a few friends toasted us with champagne-filled plastic cups, and we then walked down the street in search of a diner for breakfast. For the rest of the day we spontaneously wandered around New York City in a happy daze. Our punk-rock-activist friend gave us an architectural tour on our first Staten Island ferry cruise to get the best free view of the skyline. He then left us at the foot of the Brooklyn Bridge with walking directions.

We attracted a lot of attention dressed in our wedding attire. Arm and arm, with a crown of flowers on my head and a bright bouquet in my hands, I felt like a two-person love parade. People seemed to know that we had just gotten married, giving us warm smiles and congratulations as we passed. The Brooklyn Bridge footpath was like a long aisle in a majestic cathedral, and everyone we passed was a guest at our wedding. I recalled the words of a man I interviewed who said when he fell in love "it was like marrying the whole world" (Love Force Man).

> 66 The minute I heard my first love story I started looking for you, not knowing how blind that was. Lovers don't finally meet somewhere. They're in each other all along. 99
> —*Rumi*

There are a handful of special days in our lives that we set aside for the sole purpose of loving. Your wedding day may take on special significance for you and your spouse for the rest of your lives. You may choose to mark your anniversary on the calendar and celebrate it with your partner with a romantic date, cards, or flowers. Sometimes people are denied the right to love, and they take matters into their own hands. This was the case in 1969 when a group of people rioted for gay rights following a police raid on a gay bar in New York, marking the start of the gay rights movement. Today the gay pride movement has created many yearly parades and festivals to celebrate LGBT (lesbian, gay, bisexual, transgender) love across the globe. But out of the 365 days in the year, I don't think there are enough days devoted to love. There are so few holidays, festivals, and commemorations when people take to the streets to celebrate—we need more of them. But we do have one national day devoted to love that we are all familiar with, Valentine's Day.

LOVE RESEARCH HOMEWORK:

Make love happen:

1. Have a love parade.
2. Play with children.
3. Compliment a stranger.

Cupid, Pull Back Your Bow

I t was the coldest February in years, and Valentine's Day burned brightly, a circle of red on the calendar promising hope, renewal, and human connection. My three-year-old nephew asked me to explain what the holiday was all about. "On February fourteenth, everyone around the world gets a special reminder to give kisses and hugs. On Valentine's Day people show each other just how much they care. You can do this in lots of different ways. You can make a card or picture that expresses your feelings. Or just spend time with the people you love. You can also invent entirely new ways to give kisses."

He interrupted me, "Like what kind of kisses can you give?"

"You might imagine how a butterfly or hippopotamus might kiss, or maybe even invent how to give someone a kiss during a snowstorm. On the holiday you can find ways to be helpful to your family. It's also nice to be extra friendly—you could say 'Happy Valentine's Day'—to people you meet on the street."

He piped in, "I like to say hello to people out the window."

"You're a friendly boy," I tell him.

"You can also wear red because that color makes people think of love. It's lucky to have a holiday that reminds us how wonderful it feels to love and be loved. Do you know all over the world people love one another, but they have different ways to say that special word? Here are some different ways to say 'I love you' in other languages. In Norway they say *Jeg elsker dig*, Germans say *Ich liebe Dich*, Spanish-speaking people say *Te amo*, and in France they say *Je t'aime*."

My nephew and I practiced saying 'I love you' in French over and over again for the rest of the day, "*Je t'aime, Je t'aime, JE T'AIME*."

LOVE RESEARCH HOMEWORK:
Invent new kisses.

Valentine Origins

Each year, as our national day of Love inches closer, signs go up all over the city, making it almost impossible to forget. Florists, jewelry stores, card shops, and chocolate makers go into overdrive stocking abundant showcases and decorating elaborate holiday displays with hearts, arrows, and paper cupids flying overhead. People make passionate purchases of roses, sparkling jewelry, and velvety boxes of dark chocolates to give to their lovers. Dates will be marked on calendars for romantic evenings out, restaurants will be booked up for the night, and troops of baby sitters will be called into service. But where did this ritual of symbolically giving hearts away actually begin?

LOVE RESEARCH HOMEWORK:
Eat chocolate.

There are varying legends surrounding the holiday, each with a slightly different tale. The ritual probably stems back to ancient times to a pastoral celebration called Lupercalia. Observed on February 13 through February 15, it was a time to avert evil spirits and purify the city, releasing health and fertility. Houses were swept clean and sprinkled with salt and spelt. Goats were sacrificed. And at the end of the day, eligible young women placed their names in an urn and unmarried men drew a name to find a bride. As Christianity came into dominance in Europe, many pagan celebrations were renamed for saints and became Christian feast days. In A.D. 496, Pope Gelasius recast Lupercalia as Saint Valentine's Day to commemorate a third-century martyr, Saint Valentine.

Most scholars agree that the martyred saint was probably a priest who fell into disfavor with Emperor Claudius II around A.D. 270. When civil strife and outside threats placed new pressures on the declining Roman Empire, the brutal emperor decreed a ban on marriage, believing that unmarried men made stronger soldiers. A priest named Valentine defied the new law by secretly marrying young lovers. When Claudius found out, he sent the love rebel to prison. While awaiting his fate, Valentine met his jailer, Asterius, who asked him to heal his blind daughter. According to legend, Valentine fell in love with her and prayed for a miracle that restored her sight. His parting love note to her, as he was taken from the prison, was signed, "From your Valentine." On February 14, 270, Valentine was stoned and beheaded and was eventually made a patron saint— and the spiritual overseer of the annual festival. In Roman times, young men offered woman they admired handwritten greetings of affection. These notes later became known as the first Valentines.

LOVE RESEARCH HOMEWORK:
Make Valentine's Day cards.

The Economics of Love

Our contemporary day devoted to love has become big business. According to an MSNBC report, Americans spent as much as $13.7 billion on Valentine's Day in 2006, up 22 percent from just five years ago. Valentine's week sales account for more than five percent of annual chocolate sales, totaling $345 million. According to Hallmark, half of the U.S. population celebrates Valentine's Day by purchasing at least one greeting card. That figures out to be around 180 million Valentine's Day cards exchanged annually, making it the second biggest holiday of the year next to Christmas. Thinking about all the money spent on Valentine's Day was overwhelming, and I decided to do things a bit more economically. I decided to write my husband a love letter.

Signed, Sealed, Delivered

Every day we communicate. Linked together through the Internet, we send e-mails to friends when we're in desperate need of a break from our office jobs, or updates to keep in touch with our families. But a genuine, bona fide love letter is not something you get every day. In our high-tech, fast-track world it's easy to forget that letter writing was once the standard form of communication and has a history dating back thousands of years. A hundred years ago, people kept careful written correspondence because it was the only way to stay in touch across great distances.

> " Romantic love is a universal human feeling, produced by specific chemicals and networks in the brain. "
> —*Helen Fisher*

The Victorian era elevated letter writing to an art form, as writers artfully scripted letters and envelopes, inventively embellishing them with decorations, flowers, or personal keepsakes. Today, people simply don't take the time to sit down with their thoughts and carefully express them on paper. Writing a letter is a slow and thoughtful process. It's a dramatic act that a writer must be fully present for. There's no multitasking while writing a love letter; it requires focus, attention, and passion. A well-written love letter is a living, breathing document that can embody a spirit of its own. When we write them we struggle to give voice to our hearts in the hopes that our beloved will heed our call.

When was the last time you received a love letter? When did you last write a letter with a passionate declaration, an urgent plea, or a simple reminder that you love someone? If you feel urgency for someone, an overwhelming passion that cannot be contained, pick up a pen and paper. Seize the inspiration! Let the words flow from the depths of your heart. If you have been married for half a century (or it just feels that way) and are stuck in a dull mindset, reflect back to a time when you felt that urgency. Take a moment and meditate. Simply conjuring these moments will put you in a perfect state to start a love letter.

If you're having trouble writing down your feelings, check out the famous love letters that follow.

To Fanny Brawne:

13 October 1819

I cannot exist without you——I am forgetful of everything but seeing you again——my life seems to stop there——I see no further. You have absorb'd me.

I have a sensation at the present moment as though I were dissolving. . . . I have been astonished that men could die martyrs for religion——I have shudder'd at it——I shudder no more——I could be martyr'd for my religion——love is my religion——I could die for that——I could die for you. My creed is love and you are its only tenet——you have ravish'd me away by a power I cannot resist.

John Keats

English writer

January 8, 1845

Monsieur, the poor have not need of much to sustain them——they ask only for the crumbs that fall from the rich man's table. But if they are refused the crumbs they die of hunger. Nor do I, either, need much affection from those I love. I should not know what to do with a friendship entire and complete——I am not used to it. But you showed me of yore a little interest, when I was your pupil in Brussels, and I hold on to the maintenance of that little interest——I hold on to it as I would hold on to life.

Charlotte Brontë

English writer (1816–1855),
to Professor Constantin Heger

November 16, 1814

My Heart——We are thus far separated——but after all one mile is as bad as a Thousand——which is a great consolation to one who must travel six hundred before he meets you again. If it will give you any satisfaction—— I am as comfortless as a pilgrim with peas in his shoes——and as cold as Charity——Chastity or any other Virtue.

Lord Byron

English poet (1788–1824),
to Annabella Milbanke,
his future wife

To Robert Browning:

And now listen to me in turn. You have touched me more profoundly than I thought even you could have touched me——my heart was full when you came today. Henceforward I am yours for everything.

Elizabeth Barrett Browning

English writer (1806–1861)

15 August, 1904

My dear Nora,

It has just struck me. I came in at half past eleven. Since then I have been sitting in an easy chair like a fool. I could do nothing. I hear nothing but your voice. I am like a fool hearing you call me 'Dear.' I offended two men today by leaving them coolly. I wanted to hear your voice, not theirs. When I am with you I leave aside my contemptuous, suspicious nature. I wish I felt your head on my shoulder. I think I will go to bed.

I have been a half-hour writing this thing. Will you write something to me? I hope you will. How am I to sign myself? I won't sign anything at all, because I don't know what to sign myself.

James Joyce

Irish writer (1882–1941)

P.S. —While I was writing the last page, tear after tear fell on the paper. But I must cheer up——catch!——An astonishing number of kisses are flying about——The deuce! I see a whole crowd of them! Ha! Ha! . . . I have just caught three——They are delicious!

Adieu——Dearest, most beloved little wife——Take care of your health——and don't think of walking into town. Do write and tell me how you like our new quarters—— Adieu. I kiss you millions of times.

Wolfgang Amadeus Mozart

Composer (1756–1791)

Pen Me a Poem

If you've tried writing a love letter in earnest and still no words will come, you may want to consider hiring a professional. A simple web search reveals hundreds of sites offering various personalized love letter services. The most inspiring site has to be Pen Me A Poem (*www.penmeapoem.com*). There, an English bard named Edward Beaman-Hodgkiss advertises the sale of love poetry. He can pen romantic lines for a vast array of occasions and subjects, and he posts a menu for you to choose from which includes: Valentine's Day, Declarations of Marriage, Declarations of Love, Wedding Anniversary (including Silver and Golden), Secret Crush, and Erotic Poetry. I thought his prices a bargain; you can order a personalized 200-word love letter for the paltry sum of twenty-five pounds ($50), and a standard love poem of twelve lines or less for just $40. Being a very literary man, he even offers more complicated poetic structures, which sound incredibly romantic and antiquated such as the villanelle, Petrarchan sonnet, rondeau, or sestina, but these prices run a bit higher.

> "Spread love everywhere you go. Let no one ever come to you without leaving happier."
> —*Mother Teresa*

Curiosity led me to contact Edward to see if he would be willing to participate in a Love Research interview. He happily agreed and even offered insights into the business of writing love letters and poems.

❧ Who are your love heroes? Who taught you love?

I don't think anyone taught me love. My parents showed me their love for me, as did my late grandparents, but love in the romantic sense was a lonely road of trial and error. My parents never loved one another and their marriage was merely to give me security. I am an only child so didn't have the lessons learned from an older sibling. I learned about love mainly from films and books and also by watching loving couples in parks and cafes. I was, and still am, a devoted reader of novels and poems. My favorite love films, which have greatly influenced my writing and which hold an attachment to me, are the Italian films *Cinema Paradiso* and *Il Postino*. The former I would class as my favorite film in existence and close to how I see love.

❧ What is love? (Define it in ten words or less.)

Love is the soothing stream that flows through the muscles and bones of your body rendering them both wonderfully at peace and joyfully vibrant. It's the unflinching gaze between eyes that harbors playfulness, but also deep desire and ferocious need. Love sits in the space between two pairs of hands clasped together, that are gently swinging, as two lovers walk down any street in the world. It's powerful enough to render breath impossible if broken, brave enough to surrender in the face of death if the loved one will be saved from danger, and strong enough to weather the rivulets of time better than any mountain known to man.

🏹 What do you love? List what you love in two minutes.

People use the word *love* with much abandon. Things people forget about within five minutes of declaring their love for that something often render the word meaningless. In that sense, I love very little. I love my parents and I love my girlfriend. I love to live also, despite the suffering if often entails.

🏹 Have you ever been without enough love?

I felt very lonely in my teenage years and early twenties. The battle to find my identity and gain confidence was a lonely path. I was a late-developer when it came to having girlfriends, probably due to always attending all-boys schools, and in my teens that created a certain kind of emotional loneliness.

🏹 What is the biggest risk you have ever taken for love?

That risk will take place in a couple of months or so from now. I will leave England and go to India to be with my girlfriend. From there,

I will continue my poetry writing for clients and probably teach English and miscellaneous freelance writing. I guess it's not a gigantic risk compared to what others have been through.

🐍 Do you think love is increasing or decreasing in the world?

No. I think it stays pretty much constant. The problems are faced in how certain cultures deal with love. Women suffer terribly in many parts of the world for just falling in love, due to their laws and customs. I think all writers, artists, poets, and those who admire, respect, and live for love, creativity, and equality must shout out against these injustices. Unfortunately, most don't and instead like to blame the West for world evils.

For the Love of Letters

A friend also put me in touch with another brilliant writer-for-hire, Samara O'Shea. She runs her own letter-writing service at Letter-Love.net where you can click on the "Order A Letter" tab to have a love note custom-made for just $50. This Valentine's Day, when Samara stopped by my booth for a Love Research interview, she also generously shared her own professional tips on how to write an effective love letter.

I first asked Samara who she thought were the best love letter writers. Since love letters never lose their potency, she often looks back in history for inspiration. "Mark Twain is actually an incredible letter writer," she said, "John Keats in his short life. Beethoven. And women, there is a short story writer named Katherine Mansfield who is a great love letter writer." Samara said inspiration to write can be found anywhere. She writes in her office, at the dining room table, or even sometimes at Starbucks. For her, the location doesn't matter, she just always needs a cup of tea to start.

I asked her if she could give me step-by-step instructions on how to write a love letter. She put it quite simply, "Write stream of conscious . . . just write and let the emotion drive you. Feel it. Then set it aside for a day, and reread it with fresh eyes cleaning up what's messy. But also don't worry too much. It's not a research paper. Make a list of adjectives to describe the person. Use the list as an outline and write a sentence or two around each word. Or quite literally it could be a list of things you love about a person with 'What I love about you' written at the top. Have fun making your list. The great thing about love letters is you really can't go wrong. Everyone loves to hear how amazing they are. It's such an easy act that really moves people," she said. "There are so

> "[Love is] a fundamental human drive. Like the craving for food and water and the maternal instinct, it is a physiological need, a profound urge."
>
> —Helen Fisher

few times in life that you get a document that is all about you. That is what makes love letters so incredible. What makes a good love letter is the intentions behind it. If you are well meaning and express something genuine, it will come through."

My curiosity about letter writing satisfied for the moment, we moved into a Love Research interview. I wanted to hear her thoughts about that many-splendored emotion.

𝓔 What is love? (Define it in ten words or less)

Love is when someone else's happiness and well-being mean more to you than your own.

𝓔 Who are your love heroes? Who taught you love?

My parents are my love heroes. Because of the way they love me, the way they love each other, and the way they love friends and strangers alike.

𝓔 Have you ever fallen in love? Describe the process.

I have been in love. It starts with attraction and infatuation—the easy part. It then takes on the characteristics of friendship, a genuine enjoyment of each other's company and honest concern for the other person's state of mind and body. After a while it becomes a balancing act, you balance your needs and those of the other person. You need to know when to put the other person first and when to put yourself first. Like life, love is a journey, not a destination. Circumstances are ever evolving and people are always changing. It's easy to love someone when it's convenient for you, the true test of love comes when you can put another person's needs before your own when it's most inconvenient.

?❧ What do you love? List what you love in two minutes.

I love cake.

I love rain on the roof.

I love the creator of the universe.

I love kind souls.

I love laughter.

I love laughing with someone.

I love my sister.

I love my mom.

I love my dad.

I love sunshine.

I love writing letters.

I love receiving letters.

I love writing in general.

I love when I have the power to help someone.

I love opportunities disguised as challenges.

I love when a song or a poem seems as though it were written with me in mind.

?❧ What is the biggest risk you have ever taken for love?

I told a man I loved him knowing that he would never say it back and knowing it might frighten him away forever. I said it because it was the truth and it needed to be told.

After listening to Samara's interview, I thought about the different risks people take for love and the different ways in which love—and the search for it—can be a risk in itself.

LOVE RESEARCH HOMEWORK:
Write a love letter.

Queen of Hearts

Risk \ risk \ *n* [F *risqué*, fr. It *risco*] (ca. 1661).

> **1:** possibility of loss or injury: PERIL **2:** a dangerous element or factor **3 a:** the chance of loss or the perils to the subject matter of an insurance contract; also: the degree of probability of such loss **b:** a person or thing that is a specified hazard to an insurer <a poor ~ for insurance> **c:** an insurance hazard from a specified cause or source <war ~ >
>
> *Source: Webster's Dictionary*

When I ask, "What's the biggest risk you have ever taken for love?" people always seemed to take a few steps back. This is understandable because when you take a risk, you put yourself in jeopardy. It's interesting that the word *risk* is derived from the Arabic word *rizk*, meaning "to seek prosperity." Its origin doesn't have explicably negative connotations. Risk just denotes the degree of probability that something will occur; the outcome could have either beneficial or adverse consequences. However, in modern usage, most of us tend to think of risk in terms of a perilous situation that will eventually lead to a loss for us.

We've become leery of the word, when we hear it our defenses go up. In love, the fear of rejection can literally stop you in your tracks. We sense that something might be emotionally risky and we retreat back into ourselves like a turtle into its shell. After going through a divorce or a painful breakup or if you've ever been cheated on or jilted, how do you keep yourself in the game? For many people I interviewed, Cupid missed his mark, leaving them cautious and restrained, and they held back in their next relationship just to avoid another heartbreak.

In many industries risk is actually calculated before important decisions are made. Risk assessors mathematically measure the probability that loss will occur for insurance companies, aircraft industries, engineers, and financial investors with formulas that can make or break policies, products, and services. When we think of risk in more personal terms, it's the uncertainty of the outcome that makes it so scary. If we had a risk assessor to give us the odds of a love-match, imagine what we might be more willing to try!

As a fledgling performance artist in school I learned that the best art always took risks. The artists who put themselves out there the most boldly and showed you something that had never been seen before, made good art. When you faced uncertain odds, looked fear in the face, and accepted that anything could happen, you no longer feared failure. Failure simply wasn't possible, because the act of putting yourself on the line, and actually taking the risk made it all worthwhile. This method can easily be applied to love. Oftentimes, fear of rejection prevents us from following our intuition and heart's lead. But if we can change our thinking to see every risk, not as an anticipated loss but as an opportunity to express the deepest part of ourselves, we will be more daring. The chance you take may not guarantee that someone will love you, but I guarantee that bravery will make you a better lover.

Read the interviews that follow for inspiration if you're thinking of taking a gamble with your heart.

street dictionary

What is the biggest risk you have ever taken for love?

I'm kind of a risk taker for love. I have moved around the world for it. I have lost everything for it. I have gained everything for it. I don't know, maybe ultimately the biggest risk and maybe the biggest joy was deciding to have children with my husband. That's huge when you decide to make that leap. You don't know how your life is going to change. How your heart is going to grow. If everything will be all right and if your child will be healthy. So that's the biggest risk I've taken for love. Our child came out of the love we have for each other.

—*Raina, Museum Educator*

I believe it was when I married my husband, thinking that he loved me and cutting off my family when they tried to warn about what he was like. . . . It's a risk that I wish I had not taken because what they were trying to tell me, and what I wouldn't listen to, was this man fit the classic profile of the batterer, and that was exactly what he did. I have renewed contact with my family, in fact I am living with my parents waiting for the final divorce papers . . . but it's a risk I wish I had not taken. I wish I had listened to those wiser than myself.

—*Softball Woman*

That is easy for me. The biggest risk I have ever taken for love is actually choosing to leave love. It happened when I was with somebody very seriously for seven years but I couldn't manage to say *yes* and walk down the aisle. Something inside me knew he wasn't the guy I was supposed to be with for the rest of my life. It wasn't that I didn't love him anymore, or he didn't love me. We were just different, and I knew I wouldn't be happy if I did stay with this love. So the biggest risk I took for love was leaving love to go find new love that would be better for me years down the road, but to this day I don't regret it for a minute.

—*Pinned Girl*

I left a relationship with someone very special. After years of struggling and working and trying to be happy, I decided I had to love myself first. No matter how hard I tried to quiet my inner voice, I couldn't get it to settle down. I realized that I could never force myself to be happy. I had to take a leap of faith and trust the voice that only I could hear. I moved out and made myself move on so that I could be open to true love, a love that my whole being could celebrate.

—*My Younger Sister*

Risk is constant in giving love. You give, in spite of fears that it may not be returned.

—*My Mom*

Unprotected Sex. I mean that is a big risk judging by today's society . . . now that AIDS and HIV are so rampant. You know, love makes you do stupid things and unprotected sex is one of the biggest risks that it makes people do.

—*Unprotected Sex Woman*

I moved continents.

—*Gina*

The biggest risk I have ever taken is to have children and to attempt to successfully model love for them.

—*My Dad*

Let's see, I fell in love with a married man and I kind of pursued him a little bit, because he was married and I knew he needed a little push.

—*Married Man Woman*

In the year I turned thirty I took a trip to Puerto Rico and fell quick and hard in love with a friend I was visiting. I decided to move down there to live with him on the beach, raising babies named Marisol and Zeus. It took a few months to pack up, and during that time I began to doubt my decision, and sadly, by the time I arrived, I was already out of love.

—*Linda*

Kissing my best friend and taking the risk to compromise that friendship; it is now a month after that happened. I had to think it through and make sure it was strong enough to compromise that friendship. It might turn into love, and it might make both of us happier than what we had for almost ten years—and so far so good.

—*Lifetime Man*

Leaving a residence to be with someone who I knew it wasn't going to work out with. Ultimately, it left me on the streets. I knew not to do it because of the person's age and the circumstances where we met—and why he was there. There's a big story behind this, but the bottom line is if you find love in a minute, it's not going to last for a long time. You have to do a little work before you get there. It's very important to learn about each other before you jump into anything.

—*Woman on the Edge*

One time we were walking across Seventh Avenue at Gramercy Park off of Park Avenue and we were so in love we were hugging in the street. When we got into the building we went in there and we were hugging and kissing and somebody could have come in and caught us. So we went into my apartment. He lived in Long Island with his ex-wife at the time. He had to get a 10:32 train home, and we walked over and my aunt and my daughter were there in my apartment. I said, "My god you can't be alone in this city!" So we went down into the basement of the building and made love on top of the washing machines. Somebody could have come by (laughing)! But they didn't catch us.

—*Broken Valentine's Day Woman*

The men and women I interviewed have shown me that people take some of the craziest risks for love, but sometimes, the biggest risks of all are the ones taken when one is looking for love.

LOVE RESEARCH HOMEWORK:

What is the biggest risk you have ever taken for love? If you haven't taken any risks lately, try one of these.

1. Serenade someone.
2. Send a love letter to a stranger.
3. Make love in a public place.
4. Adopt a grandparent.

Love Seekers

There are 46 million single women and 38 million single men over the age of eighteen in America. An unusually large number of them have found their way to the Big Apple, and nearly all of them will, at some point, find themselves in pursuit of love. Where can love be found in a city of 8 billion people? One woman I met told me, "I see love all around us." She burst out laughing, "How exciting! Everything around us can be seen through loving eyes if we see the world with compassion" (Asian New Age Woman).

However, even with love all around us, with all of these individuals seeking the same little elusive L word, there's bound to be some frustration. This goes a long way to explain the existence of Craigslist's Missed Connections, Meetup, Nerve, Match.com, JDate, and the other 21,200,000 singles' dating sites out there.

Locking eyes on the F train - m4w (last nite)

Reply to: pers-832288294@craigslist.org
Date: 2008-09-08, 10:15AM EDT

Going from 34th to Delancey. We looked at each other a few times while waiting for the train. When it arrived you were initially seated with your back to me; you looked over your shoulder and I was still looking at you. Then you got up and sat across from me (as a response?). It was chilly so you pulled out a cardigan. You carried yourself so elegantly, with a lovely blowout/fro and glasses. You were carrying a small, curious looking, faded gold leather case. Maybe it carried an instrument?

I told myself I'd talk to you if you got on the J, but you didn't. You'll probably never read this, but for everyone else who is: Why are we such cowards? Why do we give ourselves such foolish ultimatums that just foster our hesitancy? We're just strangers on the train, on the street, somewhere, anywhere. We have nothing to lose and who knows what to gain. Just talk to 'em.

Noonish - m4w - 22

Reply to: pers-832201150@craigslist.org
Date: 2008-09-08, 8:51AM EDT

I got on the 1 train at Times Square, you were already on the train.

You were wearing a dark skirt and a purple top - you had Versace sunglasses on.

I was in a black and white stripes and jeans.

I was trying to be subtle but you had the most amazing eyes.

You got off at 50th Street - so no time to flirt.

you rode a skateboard and just got something at the corner store. m4w - 27 (greenpoint)

Reply to: pers-832104863@craigslist.org
Date: 2008-09-08, 3:29AM EDT

i was the guy in the hoodie buying an orange juice.

nice maiden shirt. hi.

I don't know what it is about New York City, but there are just so many women here searching for love. Perhaps there's an overabundance of lovely ladies living here, or maybe there's a shortage of eligible, available men. One of my friends, a brilliant, artistic woman, would regularly tell me about her rough-and-tumble adventures in the dating world. She was the first brave soul I knew to try Speed Dating, and she experimented with all kinds of dating services before giving up on the North American continent entirely, setting her sights on Africa, in search of adventure and love. When I interviewed her for Love Research she shared with me a ritual she found for love seekers. I think it is valuable for anyone who would like to let more love into their life. She said:

"I was reading this book of rituals and it had this love ritual. It said to get cinnamon and all these spices, a pink candle, and pink rose petals, and you strew them all around, then you do this chant to prepare for love. The cool thing about this ritual, and the reason I mention it, is that it said *Invite love into your life*. It said do not have anyone's name in mind because they may not love you enough. Just invite love, and I think this is really true—you just have to invite it in."

LOVE RESEARCH HOMEWORK:
Read poetry aloud.

Attention is a kind of passion. What we decide to focus on is like a seed planted; it grows. The great French actress Sarah Bernhardt said, "Life begets life. Energy creates energy." I would add, *Love engenders love*. Our awareness can actually shape the world. When we are falling in love, signs of it make themselves known everywhere. When I fell in love with my husband, I remember that every morning for three days in a row I found a tiny feather lying at my feet. I picked up each one and collected them in a box believing they were signs from the universe that said, *yes, he is the one*. Everything I saw reminded me of him and the fact that we were in love. In fact, there wasn't a single thing that didn't make me think of him. He was the lens through which I saw the whole world. When we fall in love, it's like wearing rose-tinted glasses, everything is newly washed in color. In this state, even breathing air can be intoxicating.

My friend is a Virginia Woolf scholar. When she and I studied in England together we spent many drunken evenings reciting literature and poetry aloud. One of our favorites to recite was Baudelaire's wild appeal, "You must always be intoxicated," "never be sober," "use wine, poetry or virtue as you please."

> "Ask the wind, the wave, the star, the bird, the clock, ask everything that sings, everything that speaks, ask them what time it is. And the wind, the wave, the star, the bird, the clock will reply: it's time to be intoxicated!"
> —*Baudelaire*

I would make a similar plea to all who are love seekers. If you want to see love lurking in the corners and back alleys, and nooks and crannies of your city, let yourself be intoxicated by the world around you. Slip on a pair of rose-colored glasses and wander like a love detective through the city. In your search, you may suddenly notice there are signs of love everywhere that have slipped past your attention.

Follow My Heart

One fall afternoon I decided to skip a day of work with one goal in mind: *to follow my heart*. I called in sick, and spent the day looking for love. I started off in the morning by slipping on my Love Research fedora and then plugged in my iPod so I could experience the day with my own personal soundtrack. My music-loving friend became my personal DJ with a gift of an eclectic mix of romantic songs he selected to set the mood for the day. He included everything from heavy metal to Motown, punk rock to pop songs, and even some African tribal drumming thrown in the mix. I left the house giddy with Lena Horne's "It's Love" crooning in my ears. It's amazing how a little love song can transform something as simple as a walk to the subway. The soundtrack put a rosy tint on the whole ride, despite the fact that it was rush hour.

Looking around at the swell of passengers, I remembered how my husband had once described a subway car as "a metal tube filled with souls." Funny and profound in equal measures, it made me laugh. On our journeys we often take our fellow travelers' spirits for granted. We only see human bodies, forgetting what lies deeper. City dwellers live in such close quarters that we can sometimes be reduced to apathy. That day I tried to shake myself out of indifference.

I became aware of a subtle dance. With every stop the car filled up with bodies that pushed together closer and closer. Strangers pressed against me firmly as lovers, but they feigned indifference. Perhaps they feared it would be overwhelming if they actually acknowledged each other in this forced moment of public intimacy. My sweaty palm clung to a metal pole with twenty other groping hands, and some nameless, faceless person mashed up against my backside and breathed warmly into my ear. The pressure of bodies against me increased as more people tried to flatten themselves into the warm mass. I lost track of my singular body and merged with the multitude. All of this strange, forced closeness we

> The body is a kind of open circuit that completes itself only in things, and in the world.
>
> —*David Abram*

normally tolerate or simply ignore, was illuminated by an O'Jays song, "Love Train," playing boldly in my ears.

Face-to-Face with Love

The subway lurched to a screeching stop and heaving travelers were flung against one another. Doors snapped open. A desperate human mess squeezed out like toothpaste from a tube. I peeled my arms and legs back from the crowd, escaping out of the station.

I walked up Sixth Avenue to Fifty-fifth Street until I came face-to-face with a larger-than-life super-sized version of L-O-V-E. Robert Indiana's pop art sculpture was erected at this midtown corner in 1967. Since then, this bold image has stood as an image of hope for all the city's love seekers. Ironically, here on the Avenue of the Americas, Love is hedged in on all sides by commerce: Bank of America, Commerce Bank, and Citibank surround the public square. Like other New York attractions, it's bordered with street vendors: a fruit seller, a hot dog man, a halal kebab cart, and salesmen hawking knockoff handbags. Mr. Indiana sure chose the right corner to drop a mammoth ten-ton Love. Here it meets a near-constant flow of people, nearly all of them stopping for a photo opportunity. All of them, that is, except New York locals, who seem to breeze past as if a giant Love, the size of an elephant, were a common sight to see.

A gray-haired European couple stopped to pose for a picture. Standing in front of Love, they kiss at the camera's flash as if the sculpture itself was an instruction. Love had that effect on many of the people as they posed for pictures, some reminding me of the corny shenanigans of high school yearbook photos. A woman in a playboy baby-tee lovingly leaned against her beefy boyfriend, seated in between the V and the E. One ironic man grimaced a horrible face at Love as his friend laughed, snapping a pic on his iPhone. Kids clamored over Love, playing hide and seek as their mom went at it like a paparazzo. A teenage girl stuck out her tush and puckered her lips as her boyfriend captured an embarrassing photo. Few pop art images are more widely known than LOVE, with various versions appearing in sculptures, prints, and paintings. The U.S. Postal Service even featured the popular symbol on a stamp in 1973, selling 333 million of them (which I hope were used for love letters). The iconic sculpture itself has been reproduced in numerous locations worldwide and has even been rendered in Hebrew, Chinese, and Spanish. I can only imagine the infinite outcome of all those international photo sessions.

On a lonely day before my husband arrived, I stumbled onto the sculpture during a lunch break. The simple size and scale of it cheered me up. Now I tell my girlfriends, when you are looking for love in all the wrong places, and your heart feels like giving up, take a trip to Midtown to visit this heroic monument to love. Disappointment is not an option: you are guaranteed to find the LOVE you are looking for, and as a bonus, you might even get a little injection of inspiration, the necessary fuel for all love seekers.

Pygmalion and Galatea

The next stop on the love train was the Metropolitan Museum of Art, for a viewing of their extensive collection of nineteenth-century sculptures by Rodin. An orgy of marble lovers abounds in the B. Gerald Cantor Sculpture Gallery. Nude couples push together, pull apart, and twist, wrenching for one another's bodies in the agony and ecstasy of union and separation. Walking through the gallery, imagination takes hold, and the stone seems to come to life.

The first sculpture I looked at was inspired by Ovid's story of Pygmalion, who fell in love with an ivory statue he carved, inspiring the goddess Venus to transform the figure into living flesh. Rodin, like a minor god himself, carved *Pygmalion and Galatea* in 1889, transforming stone into seemingly living flesh. Rodin totally identified with sculpture as an art form. When he touched clay for the first time, he said it felt that he was ascending to heaven. His designs, he claimed, were delivered to him by divine visions where arms, heads, or feet appeared in the marble. From there he attempted to bring together the figure as a whole, "Suddenly, I grasped what unity was. . . . I was in ecstasy." Bodies looped together, limbs expanded like wings, two became one. Looking at the sculptures you cannot fully tell where one body ends and another begins. Stone adds a dimension to the embrace making them truly eternal. Lovers bound in eternity. Rodin carved stone into gods and goddesses, mythological nymphs and lovers to remind us of our loftiest human emotions and endeavors. When we look at this artwork, the mundane slips away and our spirits soar.

Looking around the gallery, I thought of all the different ways that love presents itself in the world (in music, between people, on the subway, in artwork) and realized that love is certainly a risk worth taking. I also thought about all the people who inspire us to love. Lena Horne broke hearts with her shimmering resonant love songs, Robert Indiana made love into a landmark, and Rodin carved sensuous sculptures of mythological heroes out of stone. But who are people's real-life love heroes?

LOVE RESEARCH HOMEWORK:
Where did you see love today? Make a list of all the places that love revealed itself to you.

Love Heroes

hero, *n.*

> **[1] a:** a mythological or legendary figure often of divine descent endowed with great strength or ability   **b:** an illustrious warrior   **c:** a man admired for his achievements and noble qualities   **d:** one that shows great courage   **[2] a:** the principal male character in a literary or dramatic work   **b:** the central figure in an event, period, or movement   **3:** an object of extreme admiration and devotion: IDOL.
>
> *Source: Webster's Dictionary*

People often seemed to be confused when presented with the question, **Who are your love heroes?** On the back of the card I clarified with, **Who taught you love?** What exactly is a love hero? My definition of a love hero is someone who teaches us a life lesson or becomes a living symbol of love for us. We need love heroes; those who work to bring more love into the world and show us better ways to live. When I asked people to name their love heroes there was quite a range in answers. From family to celebrities, goddesses to world leaders, love heroes can be found right in front of us if we have an open mind. Sometimes heroes don't even take a two-legged form. One woman professed to me that her *pet* was her love hero. She said her dog actually made her want to be a better person.

We all know what a war hero is—the U.S. military officially recognizes them by pinning purple hearts to their chests and sometimes erecting war monuments in their honor. But after September 11, something different happened; I witnessed something beautiful forming in Union Square. People gathered in droves and made unofficial memorials to their love heroes, all the people they cared for who had been lost. They were spontaneous, organically formed, and unsanctioned by the city. Their power was undeniable and potent. Each display was a cathartic, genuine expression of love, longing, and loss. Scattered across the square in a chaotic spread, candles of all colors burned. There were flowers, arranged in all states of bloom and decay, some in vases, others in loosely tied bouquets.

Among these small altars were letters to lost loved ones, and personal objects from the dead. A broken

> "Do not wait for leaders; do it alone, person to person."
> —*Mother Teresa*

face of a guitar with a poem written on it, a well-loved teddy bear, stuffed animals of all kinds, fallen firefighters' hats, paper origami cranes, flags, and photographs. People wandered among the memorials, read the letters, and felt the presence of loved heroes who had touched their lives who were now gone. The sidewalks were covered in passionate chalk-written words. On the base of a war memorial, a statue of a general on a horse, was antiwar graffiti saying LOVE LOVE LOVE LOVE one another. No War. Peace. I wish that some of those homemade memorials could have remained in Union Square to remember those special people in a more personal way.

When we think of the word *hero* we think of actions that are extraordinary, beyond the every day. But love heroes are defined by small, but brave acts of expression. They do not have to risk life and limb, but they have to express themselves, put their hearts on the line. There are an infinite amount of small acts that can be achieved every day by literally anyone; in my mind that is exactly what love heroes are made of.

Stranger Love

Yesterday, coming home on the subway, I had one of those rare New York moments. Standing in a crowd at rush hour suddenly didn't feel oppressive. All my anxiety and fear dissolved, and I didn't feel like

> Love is the will to extend one's self for the purpose of nurturing one's own or another's spiritual growth. . . . Love is as love does. Love is an act of will—namely, both an intention and an action. Will also implies choice. We do not have to love. We choose to love.
>
> —*M. Scott Peck*

fleeing anymore. For an instant, I looked around and felt grateful to be sharing the space. As my eyes scanned across the wildly diverse faces, all their individual beauty shined through. I felt a tingling sensation, like it might actually be possible to love them *all*. Maybe each person on the train was actually somebody else's love hero. Our hearts might have far more potential than we realize.

street dictionary

🐾 Who are your love heroes? Who taught you love?

My parents. They are *the* definition of love after forty-five years, four kids, and everything else. A war was in there somewhere, too. They are 100 percent my love heroes and they are the ones who taught me love. They are everything I want to be in terms of love and a relationship for whoever the lucky fellow is. . . . They're a real team, and they are seventy! My mom is like seventy and my dad is seventy-seven and they still walk down the street and hold hands. It's so cute.

My other love hero . . . would have to be my dog. She's awesome. She just loves everyone. She's got a great attitude. She's never in a bad mood—and that's a love hero. You know it's so weird, I see how she is and I know it's an animal operating with a human but I have seen her operate with other animals. When another dog runs over, she is so sweet. She's got the best energy and spirit. It totally influences me and makes me want to be a better person because she is such a great dog.

—*Love Pinned Girl*

My love heroes would have to be Humphrey Bogart. They'd have to be Superman. They'd have to be Clark Gable. They'd have to be John Lennon.

—*Superman*

I would have to say my sweetheart of fifty-six years. My parents and my savior taught me to love. So who taught you to love? It's a God given gift and you have to share it. Love is forever.
—*Grandma Day (in a wheelchair dressed in flowers from head to toe)*

My father, he reminded me when he was dying that Life is a book of volumes three: the past, the present, and the yet to be. The past is over and done away, the present we're living day by day, and the future is not set you see. And that's the way it's meant to be. Life is a walk in faith.
—*Michael Day (son of Grandma Day also in a wheelchair)*

My parents count the days they were married, so they can tell you how many thousand hundred. Every day. If I called my father right now he could tell you it was 10,382 days or whatever. He keeps a tally in his datebook.
—*Confused about Love*

Once I saw a picture of Timothy Leary after he died, and it was a picture of him and his wife in their bed. On the back of the headboard they wrote kind of like kid's graffiti in crayon or something. It said—I forget his wife's name—"Timothy and Mrs. Leary forever." It was really pretty, so I think they're probably my love heroes.

—*Karen*

My parents loved being together. I remember the night they returned from a rare evening out. They had just seen the new musical *The King and I*. They danced around the kitchen table and sang the tunes together all night. Grandma and Grandpa Sorensen also loved to travel together to Mexico. They gave us tickets for our wedding so we could experience traveling there too. They were generous with love and we felt that strong giving and sharing on all sides of our world. Of course, Grandma was the great giving love we all grew up with. She was a second mother to me and really modeled loving in every way.

—My Mom

Natalie Wood.

—Drunk Natalie Wood Man

Susan Sarandon is my first choice for president. She's very lovely, she's a mother and activist and she's talented. We need a nonpolitician to rule the country. I think women should rule the country and men should do the dishes. My younger sister, when I came out with HIV, she was the only one that could deal with it without just kind of being blank. She totally came to my emotional rescue. For my birthday she gave me a star in the Perseus constellation and it made me feel important at a time when I was feeling very vulnerable. She is my deepest expression of love.

—Star Man

Currently my biggest love hero in the mass media is Rosie O'Donnell, since she came out and now everyone knows who her girlfriend is. She has kids and she's a mother, she's cool too. You know she's got the whole love thing going on.

—*Plato Girl*

Mine would probably be Mae West because in her time she was so bold and brazen and an activist for political rights, and she showed the world "Love yourself, your sensuality, and don't let anyone get in your way."

—*Carousel Girl*

Wonder Woman, Cleopatra, and my mother.

—*Ditto Woman*

Johnny Cash and his wife definitely.

—*Ejaculation Man*

My wife as we learned to love together; she birthed our amazing children and continues to patiently help all our love to grow. Our parents: Stanley, Elizabeth, and Donald, Dorothy, and our relatives from Europe who contributed their dreams, languages, and cultures to our collective family gene pool, which so enriches our family. My children who must make their own peace with the love of their mates, their family members, and, most difficult, with the love of their parents.

—*My Dad*

My Mom's unconditional love for me is part of the foundation of my being.

—*Linda*

My child, my son is teaching me love. All children are our teachers, our guides. . . . We need elevation and preservation of their purity, wisdom, and innate knowledge. Children are the light of this world, the future. I believe if there was anyone to lead us to show us the path it would be only children and the child within each of us.

—French Miracle Woman

I think little kids are generally my love heroes. They're just ready for people to love them 'cause they have no questions about their self-love. When they feel something for someone they just do it.

—I Got a Lot of Love Woman

My parents and grandparents, siblings, aunts, uncles, cousins, teachers, artists, writers, friends, pets, plants, and nature.

—My Elder Sister

I guess the Buddha taught me love, a kind of love, loving kindness. Others taught me the more down-to-earth kind of love. There have been a great many people: a woman in Holland, many male lovers I have had, and one great elder poet named Robert Duncan, who I had an affair (sobs) with thirty years ago.

—Crying Man

Daisy Bell taught me love. She's a miniature elephant and she escaped from the circus and now she's sitting on my lap and she taught me love.

—Woman Holding a Small Poodle

Muhammad Ali, Gandhi, and many strong powerful women. To make a world statement is truly heroic.

—*The End of Love Woman*

Mama and Papa, Grandma and Grandpa, Aunt Karen, Grandma Sue.

—*Three-Year-Old Kai*

I read this story about Aphrodite and she's pretty cool. She's the goddess of love, and she can put spells on people to make things better or worse. When she's mad at someone she can make them fall in love with a chair.

—*Teen Goddess*

There are some great souls on the planet doing some very important work. We are living in times where we're so lucky. There is so much connection and spiritual evolution happening right at this moment. . . . There is a spiritual leader named Amma from India who hugs everyone, and her work is so wonderful. It's brought so many people together and has opened people's hearts. Just recognizing that we are loving beings—the joy and gift of love is in us.

—*Asian New Age Woman*

Give Back Your Heart to Itself

Who are my love heroes, you ask? All the people in my life are my love heroes. My husband, parents, siblings, in-laws, relatives, and friends are all teachers who I learn from every day. Further beyond that, anyone who I interact with in my daily life can offer a lesson; sometimes, even a tense exchange on the subway can teach.

One of my early love heroes was my dad. On a hot summer day when I was around seven years old, he asked me to round up the neighborhood kids. When we got to our backyard he announced that we were all going for ice cream. A pack of us climbed into our rusting station wagon and headed to 31 Flavors, where we each received a cone. There was no reason, it wasn't a holiday, and it was done without explanation. It made a huge impression on me. I realized my dad cared about all the kids in the neighborhood. He had his own children but he didn't just take us for a special treat. Instead, he invited the whole block to join in. I remember feeling that suddenly the whole neighborhood was my family, and I should treat them that way. It's funny how the smallest acts can be heroic. I've tried to take that feeling of the world as family with me throughout my life.

LOVE RESEARCH HOMEWORK:
Open a free ice cream stand.

> **When the true light appears, the entire planet turns to face it.**
>
> —*Tao*

Every time I interview a stranger, I try not to judge. I give each person my undivided attention. I open my heart unconditionally. When I ask the person about love, he or she answers. Then something I never expected happens. The boundaries between us dissolve. Standing before me, the spirit of the person is revealed, and what I see is *love*. My brother motivated me to go out into the streets to learn this. I decided I should interview the person who inspired my quest.

What is love? (Define it in ten words or less)

Love, ultimately, may be your true state of being. On some level, we seem to be peaceful beings, and we *are* love. Beyond that, beyond the esoteric, but equally real, love seems to be a connection binding everything, but in particular just two beings who are *in love*.

Many have experienced, at some point, a true feeling of unity, possibly merging with the beloved, but love seems to be a conscious act. Like everything we think, say, or do, love seems to be a decision. A decision to recognize what might be our true nature and to celebrate it by treating the beloved, and thus ourselves, with the highest, most uncompromising faith and devotion each moment, in the moment, forever in *the moment*.

In loving—you sacrifice everything to the beloved.

ﻬ What do you love? List what you love in two minutes.

I love myself. I think that we are all interconnected and I love this universe with that knowledge. I love my family, my parents and three sisters, my loving grandma, my friends.

ﻬ Have you ever been without enough love?

It feels that way sometimes, but it is really never far. When I was in the depths of delusion and darkness I heard a voice ringing loud, as if echoing through a cathedral. That voice was the voice of my sister Karen. It said, "We love you!"

ﻬ Where did you see love today?

I saw it in my coworkers. I heard it in people's voices.

ﻬ How does one prepare for love?

By turning inward.

After interviewing my brother, I thought again about how much my family means to me and how much love each and every one of them has injected into my life. To me, my family is a true embodiment of love.

LOVE RESEARCH HOMEWORK:
Who are your love heroes? Who taught you love? Make a list of those people and let them know how important they are to you.

Dance Me to the End of Love

As a child I remember feeling overwhelmed by love. It wasn't a romantic sort of love, but a bubbling passion for being alive that percolated inside of me. It simmered up to the surface and spilled over my edges, sending my emotions in puddles all over the floor. In extreme moments I would get so excited by my feelings that I would raise my clenched fists up to my face, pressing them against my cheeks to keep from bursting apart with joy. My older sister teased me. It was funny and melodramatic, and a little embarrassing, but I remember life felt that intense at times.

I remember small things, like going to bed at night and having to choose a stuffed animal to sleep with. My sister and I collected them. We had a shelf that went all the way up to the ceiling that was filled with a menagerie of fuzzy mammals. Every night I had to pick out an animal to come to bed with me. And each time, I would see all those little button eyes pleading to be held. Each one of them looked like they wanted to be chosen for a reassuring cuddle. I knew they would all prefer to spend the night in my warm bed instead of sitting lonely on the shelf. It was always a grueling decision, and inevitably I would take armfuls of them under my covers, unable to pick a favorite. After I chose my stuffed animals, every night before I went to bed, I repeated "Good night, sweet dreams, I love you" to my parents. It was like a mantra that calmed me down, put the world to right, and allowed me to sleep peacefully.

The word *love* was commonly used in my family, spoken at the end of every telephone call and often said in greeting and parting. My grandmother's signature is always prefaced by "luv ya" and to the family it is her personal slogan. The expression sums up my grandmother's life: she revels in love and affection. I cannot think of any person who enjoys a kiss or an embrace as much. Her whole spirit seems to vibrate with love when she's giving or receiving it. While hugging you, she exclaims, "I'll squeeze the dickens out of you," and she means it. She has a surprisingly tight, viselike hold for a ninety-seven-year-old woman. Strangely, her parents never spoke much about love, and rarely if ever said *Szeretlek*, "I love you" in Hungarian. They were immigrants who most likely were never fully comfortable with the English language. Maybe they believed love was to be shown through your actions and devotion to the family, and not put into words. They weren't a physically demonstrative, close-knit family, so my grandmother must have decided to do things very differently when she had her own children. She dared to use the word *love* often and bestowed it on her children so frequently it became a common expression. She reveled in affectionate embraces with her children, family, and friends and, much later in life, nursing home attendants. I think she was making up for all those years without enough loving touch. My grandmother's wild yearning and revelry in affection have been inspirations for everyone in my family.

Recently, I went home to see my grandmother, who, at age ninety-seven, is coming closer to the end. In the year and a half since I have seen her she has aged so much—a dramatic physical transformation. The vitality of her body was nearly gone, but her spirit was still thriving. Her sense of humor and warm open smile cracked open her tired face.

I know that soon I'll have to find a way to let her go. I'll have to release her to the universe. You can't hold on to someone forever. I talked to my brother, and he told me that I shouldn't fear. He said she is going to a better place. *"There is no such thing as dying. There is not an end."* I can't help but think that the love my grandmother has will continue on after her death; it's so profound and infinite that it is a mystery inside a mystery. Her love is a force of nature as big as the wind and the sea or the cycling

> In writing we end a sentence with a period. Before starting the next one. Death is like that period. It doesn't mean an end; we just go on to the next thing.
>
> *—Amma, Mata Amritanandamayi Devi*

seasons. The love she has will never end. It will go on and on like a force let loose into the world: a wild yearning and passionate love till the end of time.

We were all sitting in my grandmother's room looking at photo albums, remembering old times, and I saw her sitting there quietly with an inward focus, slightly disconnected from the present moment. I felt like she was slipping away from us, but then she gave me a wink. It's something I realized I had picked up from her. I often give winks of reassurance to people. It always made me feel like she was watching out for me and we had a little joke between us. My grandmother's eyes spoke volumes. The wink was short for "luv ya," and I knew that she would love us unconditionally forever. It's the only thing that really matters.

When it was time to leave, we didn't want to say goodbye; neither of us wanted to admit that this might be the last time we would see each other. I gave her a giant embrace and she "squeezed the dickens" out of me like she used to say. She didn't want to let go. I gathered up my things. She held her arms open and asked for another hug. I thought about romance movies when lovers can't stop kissing goodbye. It made

> " When a man dies, what does not leave him? . . . The voice of a dead man goes into fire, his breath into wind, his eyes into the sun, his mind into the moon, his hearing into the quarters of heaven, his body into the earth, his spirit into space. "
>
> —*Brihadaranyaka Upanishad*

me laugh. We fell into each other's arms again, and it was pure love, a kind I have only felt a few times in my life. A radiant love that filled my whole body, poured through me, and flooded me with joy and bliss. It was an embrace that I imagined was as close to LOVE as it gets. I never wanted to leave it.

If I can keep the memory of my grandmother alive, it will only be through love—giant acts of love. It will be a love that is inclusive and big enough to share with all the people that will ever cross my path. It will be a love that makes everyone I meet part of my family. It will be a love that spills out and is offered to everyone. It will be a love letter to the world, an embrace for all the world's citizens.

LOVE RESEARCH HOMEWORK:
Share a slow dance with someone you love.

✒ Do you think love is increasing or decreasing in the world?

Love is infinite, a circle.

—*My Elder Sister*

I think love would increase if people had a minute to be with each other without being afraid. I think fear is the biggest thing that prevents love. If you're full of fear you don't have time to feel love. You have nothing but that worried and tense feeling all the time. I think love is always there. I think every day people are more aware of love. I just think it's harder for some to recognize this because so many factors get in the way.

—*Fourth Woman*

Love and trust go hand in hand. Trust in the world is declining and people start to get hurt over and over. Then it's harder for them to be as open and free with love. So maybe some people do hold back. I think our society has something to do with how much love we are giving off.

—*Sweet Laura*

Love is increasing every minute. Our population grows and people are great lovers of each other and their world.

—*My Mom*

I think, at their core, people are looking for love, acceptance, and the permission to completely give themselves over to something outside of themselves. I think that is always constant. But somehow, as a world, we are beginning to think doing things in an unloving way is okay, commonplace, and it doesn't demand that we all stop and scream and say, "Absolutely not!"

—*Art Educator*

Well, there's more people in the world, so there's more love in the world. It's natural. Everybody needs it. If they don't have it, they'll seek it.

—*I Love Simple Things Man*

That's hard for me to say, since my contact with the world is limited. I have traveled extensively in the U.S. and abroad, but you have to take a look at what is happening in the world, all the events. There are lots of expressions of hate; hate is the opposite expression of love. So you ask yourself, what is causing these people to be so destructive? In respect to the AIDS epidemic and cancer, it's so political, so monetary. It makes you wonder. We have this innate capacity to love others, but when you see this destruction and negativity it raises the question: Do the people who are in charge actually love? Are they capable of loving a human being, or just dollar bills?

—*Animal Rescuer*

Of course love is decreasing because so much is going on around you. You find that people are killing their children, their husbands, their wives. Around the world there is chaos. There are not enough jobs, not enough health care, not enough food, and people are homeless. If there was enough love in the world there would be an abundance of everything. People wouldn't be against one another. They would be embracing each other, you know? If I needed help putting on my coat, someone would run to my rescue. It's all about serving each other. Whoever you are, whatever color, it doesn't matter how much money you have, or even if you don't have any. It's all about us coming together in this life as *one*, that's how we're gonna make it.

—*Deb Howse*

Love is increasing. If you show love to others, they'll show love back to you. Love is forever and ever (she breaks into giggles).

—*Grandma Day*

It can only be increasing. There are those who would say that the universe is dying and the world is growing dark. I saw on TV that scientists who study "dark matter" believe that the universe can only be expanding, that eventually the entire universe, including the smallest parts of subatomic particles, will explode. To me, the earth is at a tipping point, and only the destruction of false boundaries between beings can and will save us, through love. Love is like dark matter, you can't see it, it seems to be nonexistent at times, but it will expand forever until the universe is transformed by it.

—*My Brother*

No two people feel the same way about love. But as you can see, everyone seems to want to talk about it. One thing I learned from my years of research, learning to love is a lifelong process. This book is just a beginning for me and for you. What small thing can you do today to increase the love in the world?

LOVE RESEARCH HOMEWORK:
Do you think love is increasing or decreasing in the world? Make a flag for love. Hang it somewhere to be seen.

Afterword

Love Research continues to evolve as an ongoing project, and you are invited to participate. Please use the questions in this book to inspire your own investigation. Also, look for my Love Research booth in your city, as I may be coming soon to a park near you.

WANTED

Calling all Love Seekers; Don Juans; Lonely Hearts; Virgins; Smooth Operators; Old Maids; Sex Kittens; and Anyone Lost, Jilted, or For Whom Cupid Missed His Mark.

Come and find me in the park.

All are welcome, whether you are a swinging single, recently divorced, or have been married for forty years.

I am waiting to hear your story, in exchange for one red rose.

---

100 Ways to Increase Love in Your Life

Now that you know about my love research and have heard how others feel about love, I hope you can find a personal way to help love expand in our world. If you're not sure how to increase love in your own life, try one of these options.

1. Smile at strangers.
2. Donate blood.
3. Give flowers away.
4. Skinny-dip.
5. Spread love graffiti.
6. Send a love letter to a stranger.
7. Research love.
8. Test the affects of kisses on the body.
9. Have a love parade.
10. Dress wildly.
11. Flamenco dance.
12. Ask scientists questions about love.
13. Broadcast love songs around the city.

> " No man is an island, entire of itself; every man is a piece of the continent, a part of the main. "
>
> —*John Donne*

14. Carry a kiss sign in public.
15. Hold a love symposium.
16. Read Plato's *Symposium*.
17. Make Valentines.
18. Experiment making kiss marks.
19. Write a love letter.
20. Research the heart.
21. Collect love songs.
22. Buy a love outfit.
23. Dance a tango.
24. Send a thank-you letter to a love hero.
25. Compliment a stranger.
26. Look for signs of love.
27. Buy an outrageous mirror.
28. Walk barefoot on grass.
29. Volunteer.
30. Keep a journal of where you see love.
31. Call a DJ and dedicate a love song.
32. Read famous love letters.
33. Abstain from touch for a week—write about it.
34. Write a love letter to the world.
35. Turn your bed into a sacred space.
36. Scatter rose petals.
37. Adopt a grandparent.

> 66 The only thing that lives forever is love. 99
> —*Elizabeth Kübler Ross*

38. Open a free ice cream stand.
39. Play with children.
40. Wear red.
41. Spend the day telling everyone you love that you love him or her.
42. Invent new kisses.
43. Make a baby.
44. Learn to appreciate something your lover loves.
45. Bake a cake for someone you love.
46. Give away something you love.
47. Plant seeds.
48. Plant flowers.
49. Forgive an enemy.
50. Give a massage.
51. Invent a new term of endearment.
52. Burn a mix of love songs, and mail it to someone you admire.
53. Wash your lover's hair.
54. Read poetry aloud.
55. Find new things, not on your list, to love.
56. Serenade someone.
57. Pet animals.
58. Paint a room red.
59. Practice giving.
60. Practice receiving.

61. Open your windows.
62. Donate to street musicians.
63. Take yourself on a date.
64. Buy dancing shoes. Use them.
65. Bake bread.
66. Invent your own perfume.
67. Bathe ritually.
68. Travel around the world with an open heart.
69. Make love in a public place.
70. Pamper your skin.
71. Listen.
72. Hold someone.
73. Share a meal.
74. Give your time.
75. Open your home to visitors.
76. Sleep under the stars.
77. Listen to love songs.
78. Pursue sensual adventures.
79. Make a love shrine.
80. Plant flowers near a family grave.
81. Make a family tree.
82. Make a family cookbook.
83. Start a Love Research book club.
84. Visit public art.

> "Know the self to be sitting in the chariot, the body to be the chariot, the intellect the charioteer, and the mind the reins."
>
> —*Veda Upanishads*

85. Lie topless in the sun.

86. Go swimming with your dog.

87. Wash someone's clothes and fold them perfectly.

88. Discover new food.

89. Paint a portrait of someone you love.

90. Rock a baby to sleep.

91. Meditate.

92. Share your favorite books.

93. Listen to your lover's heart.

94. Learn to love your body.

95. Hold hands.

96. Say yes to magic.

97. Eat chocolate.

98. Sing to yourself.

99. Take dance lessons.

100. Get married.

> "We are all involved in the single process. Whatever affects one directly affects all indirectly. We are all links in the great chain of humanity. We have before us the glorious opportunity to inject a new dimension of love into the veins of our civilization."
>
> —*Martin Luther King Jr.*

Sources

Abert, Hermann. *W. A. Mozart*. New Haven, CT: Yale University Press, 2007.

Abram, David. *The Spell of the Sensuous*. New York: Vintage Books, 1997.

Ackerman, Diane. *The Natural History of Love*. New York: Random House, 1994.

Anderson, Jon Lee. *Che Guevara: A Revolutionary Life*. New York: Grove Press, 1997.

Austin, J. L. *How to Do Things with Words*. Cambridge, MA: Harvard University Press, 1975.

Barks, Coleman. *The Essential Rumi*. New York: HarperCollins, 1995.

Baudelaire, Charles. *The Painters of Modern Life*. London: Phaidon Press, 1995.

Baudelaire, Charles. *Baudelaire, Selected Writings on Art and Artists*. New York: Penguin, 1972.

Baudelaire, Charles. *"The Flowers of Evil" and "Paris Spleen."* Ann Arbor, MI: University of Michigan Press, 1991.

Bible, Revised Standard Version. New York: Thomas Nelson & Sons, 1953.

Browning, Robert. *The Major Works.* Adam Roberts and Daniel Karlin, eds. London: Oxford University Press, 2005.

Buchanan, Scott. *The Portable Plato.* New York: Penguin, 1976.

Byron, George Gordon. *Byron's Letters & Journals.* Leslie Marchand, ed. Cambridge, Mass: Belknap Press, 1975.

Cather, Willa, *Death Comes for the Archbishop.* New York: Vintage Books, 1990.

Cave, Nick. *"The Secret Life of the Love Song" and "The Flesh Made Word": Two Lectures.* King Mob, KMOB7. CD, 1996.

Coelho, Paolo. *The Alchemist.* San Francisco: HarperCollins, 1995.

Cohen, Leonard. *The Essential Leonard Cohen.* Sony, B00006NSH8. CD, 2002.

Cummings, E. E. *95 Poems.* New York: Harcourt, Brace, 1958.

Darshan: The Embrace. DVD. Directed by Jan Kounen. New York: IFC, 2006.

Deng, Ming-dao. *365 Tao: Daily Meditations*. New York: HarperOne, 1992.

Donne, John. *No Man Is an Island*. London: Souvenir Press, 1988.

Dwyer, Jim. "What the Search Engines Have Found Out about All of Us," *New York Times*, December 10, 2008.

Fisher, Helen. *Why We Love: The Nature and Chemistry of Romantic Love*. New York: Henry Holt, 2004.

Fromm, Erich. *The Art of Loving*. New York: Harper & Brothers, 1956.

Gandhi, Mohandas K. *Gandhi on Non-Violence: Selected Texts from Gandhi's "Non-Violence in Peace and War."* Thomas Merton, ed. New York: New Directions, 1965.

Gibran, Kahil. *The Prophet*. Hertfordshire, UK: Wordsworth Classics, 1997.

hooks, bell. *All About Love*. New York: HarperCollins, 2000.

Hughes, Langston. *The Official Works of Langston Hughes*. Columbia: University of Missouri Press, 2001.

Keats, John. *Selected Letters*. London: Oxford University Press, 2002.

King, Martin Luther. *Strength to Love*. Minneapolis, MN: Augsburg Fortress, 1981.

Krishnamurti, Jiddu. *On Love and Loneliness*. San Francisco: HarperCollins, 1993.

Kübler-Ross, Elizabeth. *The Wheel of Life*. New York: Simon & Schuster, 1998.

Kulasrestha, Mahendra. *The Golden Book of Upanishads*. Twin Lakes, WI: Lotus Press, 2006.

Lacan, Jacques. *Feminine Sexuality*. New York: W.W. Norton, 1985.

Leigh, Eric Schmidt. "The Commercialization of the Calendar: American Holidays and the Culture of Consumption, 1870–1930." *Journal of American History* 78, no. 3 (December 1991): 890–98.

Lennon, John. *Peace, Love & Truth*. EMI, B000AD241A. CD, 2005.

Lifton, Robert J., and Nicholas Humphrey. *In a Dark Time*. Cambridge, MA: Harvard University Press, 1984.

McGeehan, Patrick. "State's Unemployment System Buckles under Surging Demand," *New York Times*, January 6, 2009.

Merton, Thomas. *The Wisdom of the Desert*. New York: New Directions, 1970.

Milani, Joanne. "Love from New York," *Tampa Tribune*, April 2004.

Miller, Henry. *From Your Capricorn Friend*. New York: New Directions, 1984.

Mitchell, Stephen. *The Enlightened Heart*. New York: HarperCollins, 1993.

Néret, Gilles. *Rodin: Sculptures and Drawings*. Los Angeles: Taschen, 2007.

Nevergold, Barbara A. Seals, and Peggy Brooks-Bertram. *Go, Tell Michelle: African American Women Write to the New First Lady*. Albany: State University of New York Press, 2009.

O'Donohue, John. *Anam Cara: Spiritual Wisdom from the Celtic World*. London: Bantam, 1997.

O'Shea, Samara. *For the Love of Letters: A 21st-Century Guide to the Art of Letter Writing*. New York: Collins Living, 2007.

Pausch, Randy. *The Last Lecturer*. New York: Hyperion, 2008.

Peck, M. Scott. *The Road Less Traveled*. New York: Simon & Schuster, 1978.

Peters, Margot. *Unquiet Soul: A Biography of Charlotte Bronte*. London: Hodder and Stoughton, 1975.

Rilke, Rainer Maria. *Letters to a Young Poet*. New York: W.W. Norton, 1993.

Ronan, Gayle. "Businesses Loving Valentine's Day Ever More." MSNBC.com, February 2006.

Roskill, Mark. *The Letters of Vincent Van Gogh*. London: Flamingo, 2000.

Royko, Mike. *One More Time: The Best of Mike Royko*. Chicago: University of Chicago Press, 1999.

Sagan, Françoise. *Dear Sarah Bernhardt*. New York: Henry Holt, 1988.

Sampat, Payal. "Last Words [extinction of languages around the world]," *World Watch*, May 2001.

Scholes, Robert. *The Cornell Joyce Collection*. Ithaca, NY: Cornell University Press, 1961.

Seaton, Beverly. *The Language of Flowers: A History*. Charlottesville: University of Virginia Press, 1995.

Stewart, Amy. *Flower Confidential.* New York: Algonquin Books, 2007.

Stone, John. *The Reference Dictionary of Latin Quotations.* New York: Routledge, 2005.

Strickland, Bill. *Making the Impossible Possible: One Man's Crusade to Inspire Others to Dream Bigger and Achieve the Extraordinary.* New York: Broadway Business, 2007.

Teresa, Mother. *Love: A Fruit Always in Season.* Ft. Collins, CO: Ignatius Press, 1987.

Uchitelle, Louis. "Jobless Rate Hits 7.2%, a 16-Year High," *New York Times*, January 10, 2009.

U.S. Census Bureau. "Valentine's Day: February 14," *U.S. Census Facts for Features*, February 7, 2006.

Webster's Ninth New Collegiate Dictionary. Springfield, MA: Merriam-Webster, 1986.

Whitman, Walt. *Leaves of Grass.* New York: Modern Library, 1993.

Whitman, Walt. *Song of Myself.* New York: Courier Dover, 2001.

Wilde, Oscar. *An Ideal Husband.* Upper Saddle River, NJ: Pearson Education, 2003.

About the Author

Karen Porter Sorensen is a writer and performer who has dedicated the last seven years of her life to researching love. She is a member of OVO, a New York collective committed to the development of original artworks. Her first OVO production, Love Research, presented at the Collective Unconscious, was a theatrical exploration based on six months of street interviews with New Yorkers and their views on love. This led to invitations to perform at Clemente Soto Velez Cultural Center, The Culture Project, Art in General, and PS122. As interest in the project grew and her collection of audio interviews expanded, Sorensen began work on a book version of Love Research.

Sorensen attended the University of Wisconsin-Madison, and received a BA in theater, followed by a MFA in performance at the School of the Art Institute of Chicago, where she developed numerous original performances, ranging from theatrical productions to one-woman shows, performance art spectacles, and gallery installations.

Love Research continues to evolve through Sorensen's ongoing street interviews, her scholarly investigations into the nature of love, and through her performances and public appearances. Next, she hopes to expand her project by traveling around the world to explore the subject of love internationally.